The Village Proposal

Education as a Shared Responsibility

Christopher Paslay

ROWMAN & LITTLEFIELD EDUCATION

A division of
ROWMAN & LITTLEFIELD PUBLISHERS, INC.
Lanham • Boulder • New York • Toronto • Plymouth, UK

Published by Rowman & Littlefield Education
A division of Rowman & Littlefield Publishers, Inc.
A wholly owned subsidiary of The Rowman & Littlefield Publishing Group, Inc.
4501 Forbes Boulevard, Suite 200, Lanham, Maryland 20706
www.rowmaneducation.com

Estover Road, Plymouth PL6 7PY, United Kingdom

Copyright © 2011 by Christopher Paslay

All rights reserved. No part of this book may be reproduced in any form or by any electronic or mechanical means, including information storage and retrieval systems, without written permission from the publisher, except by a reviewer who may quote passages in a review.

British Library Cataloguing in Publication Information Available

Library of Congress Cataloging-in-Publication Data

Paslay, Christopher.
The village proposal : education as a shared responsibility / Christopher Paslay.
p. cm.
ISBN 978-1-61048-059-8 (hardback)—ISBN 978-1-61048-060-4 (paper)—ISBN 978-1-61048-061-1 (electronic)
1. Community and school—United States. 2. Education—Parent participation—United States. 3. Educational leadership—United States. I. Title.
LC221.P37 2011
371.19—dc23
2011016166

For my wife Deb—who graciously put up with the writing of this book.

Contents

Author's Note		vii
Acknowledgments		ix
Introduction: The Temple Rejection		xi
1	Winter of Hope	1
2	Teachers: The Decisive Element	7
3	Spring of Despair	15
4	Teaching the Teachers	21
5	First Year	29
6	School Leaders and Supports	35
7	A Day in the Life	47
8	Family and the Community	55
9	Revelation	69
10	Multiculturalism and the Achievement Gap	77
11	Teaching Shakespeare	91
12	Policy Matters	97
13	Arrival	113
14	Politics	121
15	Later Years	133
16	Pop Culture and Technology	139
17	The Greatest Gift	155
Index		157
About the Author		167

Author's Note

Although the memoirs in this book are based on actual incidents involving real people, names and identifying characteristics of students and fellow teachers have been changed to protect privacy.

Acknowledgments

Although this book was mostly a solo endeavor, I'd like to thank all the Philadelphia public school teachers who have supported my writing over the years and encouraged me to make my voice heard; to Janet McMillan, the newspaper editor who helped me find my niche as an education writer; to my father, Dr. Charles Paslay, a 37-year veteran of the Philadelphia School District, for his blunt criticisms of the first draft of this book; to my mother, who provided emotional support; to Swenson High School's Class of 2001, who greatly improved my teaching through a trial by fire; and to Swenson's Class of 2011, who reminded me that teaching can be the greatest job in the world.

Introduction: The Temple Rejection

In the spring of 2007, a 12th-grade student of mine stopped by my classroom during my lunch period to proudly announce that she'd been accepted to Temple University and would be majoring in business the following September. She also explained that, as an incoming freshman, she had recently taken Temple's placement test and was very impressed with the fact that one of the test topics was adapted from a commentary I'd written for the *Philadelphia Inquirer*.

At the time, I wasn't aware that Temple had used my writing as a topic. I asked my student if she could recall the test prompt.

"I have it right here," she told me and produced from her binder the actual sheet with Temple's placement test topics on it.[1] I quickly scanned the paper and realized it was true: Temple had taken my article "Trashy Teen Novels Glorify Bad Behavior," published in the *Inquirer* on January 30, 2007, and used it as an essay topic.[2]

I handed the paper back to her. "Thanks," I said and congratulated her on her acceptance to Temple. She left my room, and I went back to eating my lunch, only to find I was no longer hungry. My stomach was in knots, not because Temple was using my work as a test question for their incoming freshman but because they had denied me admission to their Graduate School of Communications three years earlier.

In January of 2004, I applied to Temple, hoping to earn a master's degree in journalism. I figured I was a shoo-in. I was an experienced high school English teacher and had published several commentaries on education in both the *Philadelphia Inquirer* and the *Philadelphia City Paper*. I was a dedicated educator and had glowing recommendations from both my current principal, Dr. Reuben Yarmus, and Steve Alten, the *New York Times* bestselling author of the novel *Meg*.[3] I was also our school's varsity cross-country coach and founder of the school newspaper. In addition, I very carefully explained in my official statement of goals that I wanted a master's in journalism from Temple so I could directly pass on this new knowledge to the youth of Philadelphia.

In April, I got the one-page form letter from Temple that said I'd been rejected. The department didn't feel I was qualified. My undergraduate GPA was 2.55, and Temple's minimum standard was 3.0.

Frustrated, I decided to file a grievance. I contacted Temple's journalism department and was informed that the school's minimum standard was 3.0 and that no exceptions could be made. It didn't matter that my

GPA was ancient history—that I was a completely different person today from the immature kid who drank all that beer and cut all those classes his freshman year at Bloomsburg University 14 years earlier. It also didn't matter that I was a published writer, teacher, coach, mentor, and sponsor of the school newspaper. Temple's GPA requirement was set in stone.

This didn't stop Temple from using my writing as an essay topic for their freshmen assessment tests, however. When I became aware of this in the spring of 2007, I decided to write letters to both Dr. Ann Weaver Hart, Temple's president, and Dr. Aquiles Iglesias, the dean of the graduate school. I made it clear that if Temple was going to use my writing as an assessment tool for incoming freshman, they had better give me enough respect to grant me acceptance into their journalism program. Several weeks later, I received a letter from Dr. Iglesias—what I considered to be a second rejection letter. He explained that my writing had some merit but that, ultimately, the department didn't feel I was qualified. Specifically, I was once again told my undergraduate GPA was too low.

Flustered, I decided to tell my story on the Internet. I wrote a post on my blog describing what I felt was Temple's glaring double standard. A week later, I got a call from Morgan Zalot, a student reporter from the *Temple News* who'd read my blog. She wanted to interview me about my situation with Temple and write an article about it. I agreed. I gave her a 20-minute phone interview, and on October 30, 2007, the story by Zalot appeared in Temple's newspaper.[4] Although, in my opinion, the story was reserved and pulled punches, Zalot did a nice job of bringing some attention to the situation. She contacted Dr. Iglesias who said that the reason for my rejection was the department's decision and that "obviously the department did not feel he was qualified."[5]

Zalot also contacted Margaret M. Pippet, an assistant dean of Temple's graduate school. Pippet told Zalot that students can indeed be denied admission to the school solely based on their undergraduate GPAs. She also told Zalot that my GPA and writing skills had no relation.

"Does [writing well] elevate his GPA to the standard we need? No," Pippet was quoted as saying in the article.[6]

In the end, I was never granted admittance into Temple's journalism program.

IT TAKES A VILLAGE

In 2006, Arthur Levine, former president of Teachers College at Columbia University, authored a report about the state of teacher training in America called "Educating School Teachers."[7] One of the major findings was that education professors were disconnected from K–12 schools. Part of

Levine's study involved surveying a representative sample of 15,468 education school alumni who received degrees in 1995 and 2000.

"Some of the professors I had hadn't taught in a P–12 system for over 20 years," said one alumnus surveyed in the Levine report. "They were fairly clueless regarding the realities of the P–12 teaching environment."[8] Another is quoted as saying, "Most of the professors had no idea what was going on in today's classroom. Yeah, they may have visited a classroom a few weeks in a row or for a semester. But they don't know what it is really like until they live it day to day."[9]

Like the findings in Levine's study, my experience with Temple was an example of the disconnected nature of education today. One of the reasons I applied to Temple's graduate program was to form a bridge between their university and my classroom, to increase my knowledge of journalism so I could teach my students to be better writers and reporters and ultimately improve their ability to run the school newspaper. Yet Temple's professors got hung up on five-tenths of a percentage point and, in the process, lost sight of what education is all about.

"Education" means different things to different people. To scholars and elite universities, education is often a way to establish reputation. To politicians, it can be a way to win votes. To textbook companies, testing services, and private consultants, it's a way to turn a profit. Tragically, everyone wants a piece of "education," yet not enough end up making a meaningful contribution. And when things don't work out as planned, when the millions spent don't result in increased achievement, no one wants to take responsibility. The shortcomings of American education are always *somebody else's fault*.

The education management organization (EMO) failed to increase literacy because they weren't given enough control of curriculum by the superintendent. The superintendent failed to communicate with the EMO because he was too busy dealing with the principal's lack of leadership. The principal lacked leadership because of the lousy teachers. The teachers were lousy because of the bad parents. The parents were bad because they were working two jobs. And round and round it goes.

What no one wants to acknowledge, however, is that *everyone* is responsible for education in America. For the system to work, everyone must be focused and on the same page. The famous African proverb speaks volumes when it comes to learning: *It takes a village to raise a child*.

Education in 21st-century America is changing. It's shifted from a process-centered mentality to one of *product*. Schools are no longer measured by *how* they teach but by what they *produce*. In 2001, No Child Left Behind set the highest minimum achievement levels in history, and all public schools were held accountable. Every student—black and white, rich and poor, gifted and disabled—was expected to perform at this high level, despite their socioeconomic status, English language proficiency, mental health, or home environment.

Imagine if the government mandated that every cardiologist in America rid every patient of heart disease or face termination? What if Congress passed a law that every oncologist eradicate every tumor or be put on probation? What if they enacted a bill that forced every real estate agent to sell every house every time? This was exactly what the *no* meant in No Child Left Behind.

The vision our nation has for America's public schools in the 21st century is ambitious to say the least. This ambition is no doubt justified; every student deserves a quality education. However, to achieve this goal, to enable our nation's children to perform at the highest levels in history, we need a team effort. We need to take a *holistic* approach to education.

This idea is not new. In 1991, Geoffrey Canada started the Harlem Children's Zone (HCZ), a network of educational and social service programs aimed at reducing poverty in Harlem. HCZ, which has been featured on the *Oprah Winfrey Show* and *60 Minutes*, was groundbreaking because it took a team approach to education. The objective of HCZ, according to the *New York Times Magazine*, was "to create a safety net woven so tightly that children in the neighborhood just can't slip through."[10]

A Broader, Bolder Approach to Education (BBA), an education policy movement started by distinguished scholars and experts in the fields of education, sociology, medicine, and civil rights in late 2006, also supported a joint effort when it came to educating our nation's children. Members of BBA believed education policy was inadequate because it relied on schools alone to raise the achievement levels of high-needs children. In order to close achievement gaps, BBA reasoned, new policy must be written to include a "broader definition of schooling" and target improvements "in the social and economic circumstances of disadvantaged youth."[11] President Barack Obama agreed. In his foreword to the U.S. Department of Education's Blueprint for Reform, he writes:

> Reforming our schools to deliver a world-class education is a shared responsibility—the task cannot be shouldered by our nation's teachers and principals alone . . . . We must recognize the importance of communities and families in supporting their children's education, because a parent is a child's first teacher. We must support families, communities, and schools working in partnership to deliver services and supports that address the full range of student needs.[12]

Learning is a holistic process. For education to work, we need dedicated teachers who implement sound instruction, but we also need the guidance and support of parents. Principals must maintain an orderly school culture, while politicians must write policy genuinely aimed at improving instruction. Community leaders must make sure neighborhoods are safe and welcoming to all people, while professors must strive to stay connected to the real issues that go on inside public school classrooms. Research organizations must continue to ask the hard questions—some of which might run counter to educational trends and political correctness—and the media must hold to a standard of journalism that promotes solution-based stories on education over sensationalized half-truths that only serve to entertain the masses. As a nation, *all* of us must make education a priority.

This book attempts to analyze that very theme: *shared responsibility*. It examines the various entities that have an impact on American education and public schools. Although some elements are more influential than others, all of these affect how and what children learn.

Because teachers are the centerpiece of education, this book is also part memoir; the story of my teaching career is told in alternating chapters opposite my commentary on shared responsibility. I believe it's necessary to put my own teaching career under the microscope and lead by example. Although education is a shared responsibility, progress starts from *within*. Everyone must step up to the plate and do his or her part. This is an attitude and awareness all members of the education community—as well as society at large—must embrace.

NOTES

1. "Temple University Placement Test Topics, Form S07-C," Summer 2007, Temple University, www.temple.edu/marc/pdf%20files/Summer2007EssayTopicC.pdf (accessed August 8, 2010).
2. Christopher Paslay, "Trashy Teen Novels Glorify Bad Behavior," *Philadelphia Inquirer*, January 30, 2007.
3. I met Steve Alten after a lecture he gave at Swenson Arts and Technology High School during the 2002–2003 school year. After reading the self-published novel I'd written, he wrote me a letter of recommendation for Temple University's Graduate School of Communications.
4. Morgan A. Zalot, "Placement Tests Include Grad Hopeful," *Temple News*, October 30, 2007.
5. Zalot, "Placement Tests Include Grad Hopeful."
6. Zalot, "Placement Tests Include Grad Hopeful."
7. Arthur Levine, "Educating School Teachers," Education Schools Project, 2006, www.edschools.org/index.htm.
8. Levine, "Educating School Teachers," 45.
9. Levine, "Educating School Teachers," 45.
10. Paul Tough, "The Harlem Project," *New York Times Magazine*, June 20, 2004, 46.
11. "Who We Are," Broader, Bolder Approach to Education, www.boldapproach.org/who.html (accessed August 8, 2010).
12. U.S. Department of Education, *ESEA Blueprint for Reform* (Washington DC: U.S. Department of Education, March, 2010), 1, www2.ed.gov/policy/elsec/leg/blueprint/blueprint.pdf (accessed August 8, 2010).

ONE
Winter of Hope

In the beginning, I didn't get into teaching because I wanted to save kids. I didn't get into teaching because I believed in social justice and longed to give our nation's poorest students a first-rate education equal to their suburban counterparts. I didn't get into teaching because I hoped to inspire, or because I had a passion for working with children or because I was a privileged white kid who felt guilty about the sins of America's past. Eventually, I would establish lasting bonds with my students and get a deep satisfaction from teaching, but these things wouldn't happen until my second full-time year on the job, until I learned how to effectively manage my classroom, until I learned how to take textbook theory and translate it into meaningful instruction.

In the beginning, I got into teaching for different reasons.

I became a teacher almost by default. At 18 years old, I didn't know *what* I wanted to do; although, I had a vague interest in writing, so I figured I'd pursue English. This, in turn, led to the idea of becoming an English *teacher*. Several of my fraternity brothers were education majors, and I'd heard that education classes had manageable workloads. This sounded good to me. Plus, education courses were loaded with single women.

I was also kicking around the idea of going to graduate school and pursuing a master's degree in psychology. Because I was interested in the way the human mind worked, I figured maybe I'd become a psychologist and open my own practice. I'd get my bachelor's in education so I could teach during the day and go to school at night. That was the plan. But it didn't work out like that. I encountered a few kinks in the road. A few *potholes*. By the time I graduated Bloomsburg University with my BS in secondary education with a concentration in English, I was burnt out. It was a pathetic situation. I hadn't even started teaching professionally, and I was already tired of it.

This had a lot to do with my student-teaching experience, which, to borrow from Charles Dickens, was the best of times and the worst of times. During the spring of 1995, I interned at two different schools. Like *A Tale of Two Cities*, one encompassed the season of light, the other a season of darkness; one was a winter of hope, the other a spring of despair.

My first placement, the hopeful one, was satisfying and productive. From the middle of January to the beginning of March, I taught at Russell H. Conwell Middle School in the Port Richmond section of Philadelphia. Ironically, the school was located one block from the el train that ran above the notorious intersection of Kensington and Allegheny avenues, also known as K&A, the stomping ground for drug dealers, prostitutes, and all manner of hustlers. My cooperating teacher, Rita Donavan, a veteran teacher and native of Philadelphia, would sometimes take the el to work to save money on gas. Once in a while, she would catch her students, seventh and eighth graders no more than 13 or 14 years old, hanging around K&A after school, smoking cigarettes and curiously eyeing the underworld. Ms. Donavan would approach them, snatch the Newport from their mouths or from behind their ears, and order them off the corner with a lecture, guilting them into getting on the bus and going home.

Surprisingly, the students would nod their heads and listen, not just because Ms. Donavan was like a second mother to them but because these kids were different from your typical city yahoos. Conwell Middle School was a *magnet* school, which meant that its clientele had to go through a special admissions process. Any elementary school graduate who wanted to attend Conwell had to have standardized test scores in the 80th percentile in both reading and math, no report card grade under a B, an excellent behavior record with no recorded suspensions, and an attendance rate of 90 percent or better. Perspective students also had to attend a testing session and an interview. Competition was stiff. This, along with a dedicated administration and teaching staff, is what made Conwell one of the best middle schools in the city of Philadelphia.

My first day at Conwell, I was a bundle of nerves. I met Ms. Donavan in the main office 15 minutes before first period was scheduled to begin, wet spots at the armpits of my blue dress shirt. We made small talk—it was established that she grew up in the same Irish-Catholic neighborhood as my father—then took the stairs to her third-floor classroom. She went over some basic classroom routines and procedures and showed me to my desk. I sat down, and she gave me two textbooks—the seventh- and eighth-grade literature text she was using at the time—along with a teacher's edition of each. She also gave me an entire unit she'd complied on *The Diary of Anne Frank*, complete with interactive worksheets and videotapes of the film.

At 8:50, the bell rang. Ms. Donavan went outside to greet her students in the hallway. Shockingly, I watched as two dozen racially diverse seventh graders lined up in two single-file lines outside her door. Ms. Donavan held a finger in the air, and all talking ceased. The late bell rang, and the students entered the room and went straight to their assigned tables (four at each), took out their books, and began completing the pre-class work that was written on the board. When they finished, they waited quietly for the lesson to begin.

At this point, Ms. Donavan decided to introduce me to the class.

"This is Mr. Paslay," she said. "He will be student teaching here for the next two months. Please say hello to him."

"Hello, Mr. Paslay," the class said.

I stood up nervously. "Hello," I said. The students looked me over carefully, curiously, and I could see that they had just as many questions about me as I had about them.

On a whim, I decided to do a magic trick as an icebreaker. In my pocket, I had a red silk handkerchief and a fake thumb that would, in effect, allow me to make the hanky disappear into thin air. I had planned on doing the trick later in the week and had only brought it with me to keep at school for future use. But now, without thinking, I was waving the red scarf in the air and asking the kids if they wanted to see it disappear.

"You can do magic?" one of the students asked.

"That's right," I said. I glanced over at Ms. Donavan, and she gave me a look like she didn't want to have any part of me making a fool of myself.

"Okay," I said, "watch this." I waved the scarf one last time, and then stuffed it into my left fist. Then I held my fist up and opened it—but the scarf was gone.

"Cool!" a boy in the front said. "How'd you do that?"

"It's magic," I told him.

"Do it again!"

"A magician never repeats his tricks," I said. "But because you guys seem nice, I'll do it again this one time."

I had to briefly turn my back to the class to reset the trick. When I was ready, I faced them and once again waved the red hanky in the air, stuffed it into my left fist, and made it disappear.

"Awesome," a girl said.

I smiled, very pleased with myself. "Pretty neat, huh."

I sat back down, but the kids weren't having it. They wanted to know how I did it. To compromise, I agreed to tell them how I did the trick, but not until my last day at Conwell.

"When is your last day?" they asked.

"In March," I told them.

"*March?*"

"Yes," Ms. Donavan said. "March. Now we have a lot of work to do today, so we have to get moving. Gerald, will you go to the bookcase and pass out the textbooks please?"

Gerald got up and distributed the literature books.

I sat at my desk feeling a little looser.

REMOVING THE TRAINING WHEELS

For a week, I observed Ms. Donovan teach. I asked her dozens of questions, pumping her for information: Did she use seating charts? How long did it take for her to learn her students' names? How often did she let the kids go to the bathroom? Was it appropriate to make friends with the students? Of course, the most beneficial thing for me to do was to simply *watch* her teach.

Ms. Donovan was very good at her job. She was particularly talented at using the Socratic method of questioning to engage students and get them to think critically about the lesson and the world around them. Occasionally, she'd have a mini-debate on a current event related to the literature in the text. She might bring up the death penalty or euthanasia or school uniforms. Debates, like the ones between pundits on talk radio or cable news stations, often turned into a shouting match reminiscent of Jerry Springer, and the winner usually turned out to be the one who could talk the longest and loudest. Not in Ms. Donovan's class. She had the coveted *teacher's voice*, the one that cut through tomfoolery and sidebar conversations like lightning, and order always remained; it would take me *years* to fully develop that voice.

The first day I took over the class, I was a wreck. I was so nervous that I almost threw up before the first period bell. I didn't sleep the night before, and I kept going over my lesson plan in my head, terrified that I would get in front of the room and freeze—turn into a mumbling, stuttering zombie. It had happened the semester before during one of my education classes when I had to give an oral presentation. When it was my turn to take the floor, I had a complete meltdown. My hands shook, and my voice quaked. I could see by the looks on the faces of my classmates that it made them dreadfully uncomfortable.

The first lesson I taught at Conwell was on *The Diary of Anne Frank*. I worked closely with Ms. Donavan while developing it. For pre-class (which is educational jargon for a warm-up activity to get the students focused and on task), I brought in an article on the Holocaust and did a classic KWL activity with it. I had the students take a piece of notebook paper and fold it in three sections. The first section they labeled KNOW for the things that they already *knew* about the Holocaust, the second section they labeled WANT for the things they *wanted* to know, and finally, they labeled the third section LEARNED for the things they *learned* after reading the article.

My stomach was in knots. I remember standing up in front of the class and thinking about the slogan for Nike: *Just Do It.*

So I did.

I gave the instructions for the KWL and introduced the Holocaust. We talked about prejudice and how Adolf Hitler and the Nazis practiced racism against the Jews.

"What else do you know about the Holocaust?" I asked them. "Are there any other details? Write them down on the paper in front of you."

The students started writing. Ms. Donavan and I circulated the room, looking over the students' work and checking for understanding. Incredibly *everyone* was on task, jotting down a half-dozen responses on the K column of their papers.

"Okay," I said after several minutes. "What are some of the things we know about the Holocaust?"

A red-haired girl, who made it publicly known she was in love with Green Day, raised her hand. I still didn't know all the kids' names, so I had to glance down at my seating chart, which I carried around with me everywhere.

"Erin?" I said.

"I know Hitler forced Jewish people to wear a star on their clothes," she said.

"That's right. Jewish people were forced to wear the Star of David so the Nazis could single them out. Eventually, Jewish people were forced to leave everything behind and relocate to ghettos. Does anyone know what a ghetto is?"

A hand went up. I checked my seating chart. "Yes, Jamal?"

"A ghetto is where poor people live," he said. "Like the *hood.*"

"Yes," I said. "A *ghetto* is where poor people live. A ghetto is also an area lived in by a single race or culture. Fifty years ago, during the Holocaust, *ghettos* were sections of European cities where Jewish people were forced to live. They were cramped and crowded, like the ghetto today." I clapped my hands together. "Okay, let's move on to the next part of the activity. Look at the W section on your papers. Is there anything that you guys *want* to know about the Holocaust?"

One student was curious why Jewish people didn't fight back against the Germans, why they went to the concentration camps so quietly. Another wanted to know how the Germans were able to find out if a person was Jewish or not and if people ever lied and hid their true identity.

"These are good questions," I told them. "Why don't we read the article and see if it answers any of them."

I read the first paragraph aloud to the class. My nerves had settled. I was stunned at my confidence, which seemed to spring spontaneously from the energy of the kids and the support of Ms. Donavan.

I finished the first paragraph and looked up at the class. "Anybody want to continue reading for us?"

Hands went up like flagpoles, followed by the pleasing sound of *ooo, ooo, ooo, pick me!* I glanced at my seating chart. "Andre, would you continue for us?"

"Okay," he said.

Smiling, filled with confidence, I continued with the lesson. The training wheels were off, and I was pedaling along on my own, running the classroom, grinning from ear to ear.

TWO
Teachers: The Decisive Element

My student-teaching experience at Conwell was a success because of one major factor: *Ms. Donovan*. Although education is a shared responsibility, teachers are clearly the most important part of the education equation. Nothing sums up the power of an educator better than the words of Dr. Hiam Ginot, the schoolteacher and child psychologist who revolutionized techniques for communicating with children:

> I have come to a frightening conclusion. I am the decisive element in the classroom. It is my personal approach that creates the climate. It is my daily mood that makes the weather. As a teacher I possess a tremendous power to make a child's life miserable or joyous. I can be a tool of torture or an instrument of inspiration. I can humiliate or humor, hurt or heal. In all situations it is my response that decides whether a crisis will be escalated or de-escalated, and a child humanized or de-humanized.[1]

A teacher is indeed the decisive element in the classroom. Amid the highs and lows, the order and the chaos, how a teacher responds to his students is *everything*. Evidence continues to show that students benefit from high levels of instruction and that the most talented teachers can significantly raise their students' achievement. However, what is a "quality" teacher, exactly?

In 2010, Amanda Ripley wrote an article for the *Atlantic* that attempts to answer this question. In it, she talks about the data on student achievement complied by Teach For America, the nonprofit organization that recruits college graduates to teach in hard-to-staff schools in impoverished neighborhoods. According to the article, Teach For America used its 20 years of involvement with teaching and education to come up with identifiable attributes that great teachers possessed.

"Things that you might think would help a new teacher achieve success in a poor school—like prior experience working in a low-income neighborhood—don't seem to matter," Ripley writes. "Other things that may sound trifling—like a teacher's extracurricular accomplishments in college—tend to predict greatness."[2]

Teach For America went on to reveal that great teachers tended to set big goals for their students and were consistently looking for ways to improve their own teaching. Furthermore, great teachers worked closely with their students' families; remained focused on objectives throughout their teaching; exhaustively planned lessons by working backward from the objective; had a zest for life, which enabled them to better engage their students; refused to surrender to outside forces, such as poverty, problems with administration, and lack of resources; and achieved big, measurable goals in college, such as graduating with high grade-point averages or holding leadership positions while in school.[3]

In addition to the research complied by Teach For America, quality teachers share four additional characteristics, as noted in education consultant Charlotte Danielson's "Framework for Teaching."[4] For starters, great teachers are *strong planners and are always well prepared*. Every last thing that goes on inside the classroom is greatly affected by what goes on outside the classroom. This is the part of education that the public fails to see and understand. In American pop culture, in movies and television dramas about education, all we see is the teacher standing in front of the class, magically transforming students' lives. Rarely are we given a glimpse of all the work and preparation that goes into this feat. Teachers don't just snap their fingers, and bingo, everything they need—curriculum, equipment, materials, objectives, and so forth—appears out of thin air. They must write it *and* produce it themselves.

Great teachers also *create a classroom environment conducive to learning*. If a teacher can't control the class, it doesn't matter how well designed his lessons are; he won't be able to deliver them. In large urban districts, like Philadelphia, where class sizes can be extremely high and students suffer from a multitude of social and emotional issues, classroom environment is half the battle. For a first-year educator, depending on his talent and the culture of the neighborhood and school, it might be the *whole* battle.

In my experience, the teachers who are able to establish workable environments are those who have the ability to *relate* to their students. They develop some kind of *connection* with them somewhere along the line. Doing so is not always easy. To this day, I work with teachers who, after years in the classroom, still cannot connect with their students. They tend to talk *at* the kids instead of *to* them. As a result, tempers flare, and negative situations escalate to the boiling point.

Good teachers stay above the fray. They have a heightened awareness of confrontational situations and understand that if a student misbehaves in class, they don't have to take it personally. Most importantly, they don't have to compete with the child. They can take a step back and be a neutral observer.

In addition to being good classroom managers, quality teachers are also *dynamic instructors*. The more I teach, the more I realize that kids learn by *doing*. The best educators help their students connect the dots and draw their own conclusions. Although direct instruction is important and should drive a lesson, learning is not solely based on facts and information that teachers simply deposit into a child's brain like money in a bank. This kind of instruction, usually delivered in lecture form, is limited in its effectiveness. There are times and places for rote memorization, especially in the early grades, but as a child gets older, instruction must go deeper. Good teachers lead their students to the answer; they don't come out and give it to them.

Knowledge, no matter what subject, is like a math problem. If you give students an equation they never saw before and say, "Here's the problem, and here's the answer," and you don't teach them the process for solving it on their own, the next time they see the problem, they won't be able to solve it. You gave them the *answer*, but the answer is meaningless.

The nuances involved with this kind of instruction are subtle but make all the difference in the world. The old saying, "Those that can't do, teach," does a grave disservice to education. The craft of teaching is oversimplified by many people. This is probably because teaching feels so instinctive—it has a natural, parental quality to it. However, effective instruction is more complex than simply giving a lecture about why you should look both ways before you cross the street. To noneducators, teaching is nothing more than transferring information from one head to another. How hard can it be? Anyone who has a child in school or who has gone to school themselves knows everything they need to know about teaching, right? Not exactly. Good teaching is as much of an art as it is a science.

Not that teaching ends with instruction. Quality educators also *take care of their professional responsibilities*. Keeping an accurate and reliable grade book is no small task, neither is managing all the paperwork involved with state-mandated, individualized education plans or keeping anecdotal records on students with behavior problems or completing progress reports or calculating quarterly report card grades or completing the dozens of other forms associated with counseling, special education, and the like.

As a whole, quality teachers are well prepared, deliver sound instruction in a well-managed classroom environment, and are able to handle their professional responsibilities.

A HISTORY OF LOW STATUS

Curiously, schoolteachers don't command an overwhelming amount of respect despite performing an invaluable service to society. It's still quite common to hear the general public disparage our nation's educators, which is ironic, being that America is so intent on attracting the best people to the field.

The lack of respect for teachers may stem from the lack of respect for teacher colleges. "Since their earliest days," Arthur Levine, former president of Teachers College at Columbia University, explains in his report *Educating School Teachers*, "university-based teacher education programs have been the subject of persistent criticism and prejudice. They have been disparaged by academic colleagues for being nothing more than vocational training for women, not an intellectual matter appropriate to the university."[5]

Our country's first teacher schools were not universities but "normal schools," noncollegiate secondary schools that prepared people—mostly women with no more than an elementary school education—to teach America's children. The admission standards for these schools were low, their program of study was brief, and from their inception, these schools were attacked, as Levine notes in his report, "in the belief that others could do their job better."[6]

When accreditation came into existence and high schools began growing in popularity, higher education started taking over the role of training teachers. To compete with colleges, normal schools raised admission standards and the length of their programs and began participating in research and other activities to bolster their image and reputation. To this day, however, education departments in universities still bear the stigma of their roots.

So do schoolteachers. Educators in the 1800s—women with inferior schooling—were literally second-class citizens; women didn't earn the right to vote until 1920. Although decades have passed and education in America has changed significantly, schoolteachers still carry the lingering remnants of the "second class" label.

Unfortunately, some teachers fit the label. There is no debating that there are men and women in classrooms today who are simply not cut out for teaching. While school reformers must be careful not to oversimplify the amount of knowledge, dedication, and talent it takes to truly be a "quality" educator (not everyone is born a Jaime Escalante), there clearly needs to be more accountability in the teaching profession.

According to the United States Department of Labor, there were approximately 3.5 million teachers in America in 2008.[7] Obviously, as evidenced by national, standardized test scores and graduation rates, not all of those teachers were "quality." Interestingly, 99 percent of all teachers in the United States that year were rated "satisfactory" by their school districts.[8]

"When an ineffective teacher gets a chance to improve and doesn't," Education Secretary Arne Duncan said in his 2009 speech to the National Education Association, "and when the tenure system keeps that teacher in the classroom anyway—then the system is protecting jobs rather than children. That's not a good thing. We need to work together to change that."[9]

Quality teachers are an invaluable part of American education. Good ones must be respected and rewarded, the struggling ones should receive proper support, and those not cut out for the challenge should find a new profession. With that said, however, the attacks on schoolteachers can, at times, be unwarranted and counterproductive. The comments made by Suze Orman, the best-selling author and financial guru who was named by *Time* as one of the World's Most Influential People, is a case in point. Orman casually disparages teachers in a 2009 *New York Times Magazine* profile article.

"When you are somebody scared to death of your own life, how can you teach kids to be powerful?" she says. "It's not something in a book—it ain't going to happen that way."[10] The article goes on to explain that Orman "has been reluctant to work on school curricula on personal finance, because she says students can't learn empowerment from people who aren't empowered, and teachers, she says, are too underpaid ever to have any real self-worth."[11]

In the slick, carefully packaged documentary *Waiting for Superman*, director Davis Guggenheim does an outstanding job of disparaging teachers' unions and America's traditional public schools while advancing his own reputation and film career in the process. Not surprisingly, Guggenheim tells only one side of a very complex story.

The American news media, perhaps in an attempt to stir up controversy, have also forgotten their manners when it comes to our nation's educators. In 2010, *Newsweek* launched a full-scale attack on teachers, dedicating its March 15 issue to the campaign for their termination. On the cover of that magazine is a picture of a mock blackboard with the phrase "We must fire bad teachers" written repeatedly 11 times in chalk. In the center of the cover is written, "The key to saving American education." On the inside are several stories criticizing public schoolteachers for being ineffectual, incompetent, and inept and stereotyped teachers' unions as being stubborn and incorrigible and standing in the way of educational progress.

One story is headlined "Why We Can't Get Rid of Failing Teachers," and its title page is illustrated with a giant, red, circled F. The article opens by stating, "The relative decline of American education at the elementary and high school levels has long been a national embarrassment as well as a threat to the nation's future."[12] The article goes on to basically blame America's "failing" school system solely on teachers and notes that "teaching in public schools has not always attracted the best and the brightest."[13] The article then advocates the immediate firing of bad teachers and calls the mass termination of 74 teachers at Central Falls High School in Rhode Island in 2010 a "notable breakthrough."

Cindi Rigsbee, former North Carolina Teacher of the Year and author of *Finding Mrs. Warnecke: The Difference Teachers Make*, had a firsthand encounter with such teacher negativity in 2009 at a conference she attended on education policy. She writes about her experience on her blog:

> We weren't there long before we started feeling uncomfortable and fidgeting in our seats. Many speakers who stood before us repeatedly uttered phrases like "bad teachers" and "fix teaching." Soon we felt defensive . . . and even angry . . . and wondered what all the "teacher bashing," as one of my colleagues put it, was about. . . . A congressman who sat in a breakout session with me mentioned the inequities of technology. He said, "I saw a classroom that had only five laptop computers . . . not very effective, but more effective than a teacher in the room."[14]

Educating young people is a complex task. There are many factors involved with failure and success. Engaging lessons are difficult to write. It takes stand-up comedians months and sometimes even years to develop a successful 45-minute act, one that engages the audience and keeps their attention. Teachers must do this four or five times a day, every day, for an entire year. Jerry Seinfeld isn't that good.

Teachers are an invaluable part of a child's education. They should be held to high standards but must also be respected and treated as professionals. Doing so will help morale and improve the effort to get a quality teacher in every classroom.

NOTES

1. Hiam Ginot, *Teacher and Child: A Book for Parents and Teachers* (New York: Macmillan, 1993), 15–16.
2. Amanda Ripley, "What Makes a Great Teacher?" *Atlantic*, January–February, 2010, 60.
3. Ripley, "What Makes a Great Teacher?" 58–60.
4. Charlotte Danielson, *Enhancing Professional Practice: A Framework for Teaching* (Virginia: Association for Supervision & Curriculum Development, 1996), 3–4.
5. Arthur Levine, "Educating School Teachers," Education Schools Project, 2006, www.edschools.org/index.htm, 23.
6. Levine, "Educating School Teachers," 24.
7. United States Department of Labor, "Teachers—Kindergarten, Elementary, Middle, and Secondary," *Occupational Outlook Handbook, 2010–11 Edition*, www.bls.gov/oco/pdf/ocos318.pdf.
8. Evan Thomas and Pat Wingert, "Why We Can't Get Rid of Failing Teachers," *Newsweek*, March 15, 2010, 25.

9. Arne Duncan, "Partners in Reform" (remarks to the National Education Association, July 2, 2006), U.S. Department of Education, www.ed.gov/news/speeches/partners-reform.

10. Susan Dominus, "Suze Orman Is Having a Moment," *New York Times Magazine*, May 17, 2009, 62.

11. Dominus, "Suze Orman Is Having a Moment," 62.

12. Thomas and Wingert, "Failing Teachers," 25.

13. Thomas and Wingert, "Failing Teachers," 25.

14. Cindi Rigsbee, "Marketing Ourselves as Teachers," *The Dream Teacher*, July 13, 2009, http://thedreamteacher.blogspot.com/2009/07/marketing-ourselves-as-teachers.html (accessed October 23, 2010).

THREE
Spring of Despair

My second student-teaching placement, at Stewart Middle School in the Philadelphia suburb of Norristown, Pennsylvania, was the total antithesis of my experience at Conwell. Stewart had no special admission requirements; as long as you lived in the racially diverse, working-class west end of the municipality of Norristown, you were eligible to attend Stewart.

My first day at Stewart was a culture shock. I'd just spent a month and a half at a blue-ribbon-caliber middle school, and now I was jarred back to reality. The majority of kids at Stewart didn't score in the 80th percentile on standardized tests in reading and math, they didn't get all As and Bs in elementary school, and they certainly didn't have exemplary discipline records—not by any stretch of the imagination. The student body at Stewart had all the normal blemishes of a traditional middle school in a rough-and-tumble neighborhood: kids were diagnosed as emotionally disturbed and had a variety of learning disabilities, some suffered from Attention Deficit Hyperactivity Disorder, and they came from homes with limited parental involvement. Tragically, even at the ages of 13 and 14, too many of the kids at Stewart seemed to have lost interest in education.

The differences between students at Conwell and Stewart were evident to me immediately. So were the differences in the way my cooperating teacher, a woman named Alice Redding, who was also a veteran English teacher of many years, seemed to run her classroom. When the bell rang to begin first period, students haphazardly entered her room. As the students came in, they went to the back of the class to check their mailboxes, cardboard slots Ms. Redding had made for each student, where she returned graded assignments.

The kids retrieved their papers, most of them smiling because they received a sticker for good work. They, in turn, took this sticker and went to place it on the wall on the far side of the room. That appeared to be the ritual. If you got a sticker on your paper, you had the privilege of sticking it on the wall.

About two-thirds of the kids had one, so now there were 15 seventh graders jockeying to slap their stickers on the wall. One student, a tall boy wearing sweats with his left pant leg rolled up to the knee (that was the style at the time) was standing on the counter, trying to place his sticker as high up on the wall as he could. He actually started *jumping* on the counter to really get the sticker way up there.

It was time to start the lesson, so Ms. Redding called for everyone to be seated. Nobody seemed to be paying attention. There were still a dozen kids congregated at the back of the room, some chatting, others horsing around. Ms. Redding again called for the students to take their seats. No one moved. One boy was poking a girl in the leg with his hair pick. Another was showing his friend a song on his Sony Walkman.

"I'm going to count to three," Ms. Redding told the class. "One . . . two . . . three . . ."

I sat at my desk and watched in disbelief. It took five full minutes to get the children in their seats and another five to get them quiet enough to begin the pre-class work, which was SSR—sustained silent reading. At this point, the instructions were to take out something—anything—and read it quietly for 15 minutes. Those that hadn't done their homework and brought reading material were allowed to go over to the bookshelf and borrow something. A half-dozen kids went to the bookshelf.

The noise level for this "silent" reading was high, at least compared to the silence I knew at Conwell. There was a steady stream of conversation going on, and Ms. Redding had to keep reminding kids to sit back in their seats. A kid in the first row was sitting at his desk reading a phonebook, which he had found in the back of the room in the closet, one of those old-time, big, fat Yellow Pages.

"Shhh," Ms. Redding told them. "Focus on your reading."

Someone burped. Another cursed under her breath. It was at that moment, on the first day of my second student-teaching placement, that I lost all respect for my cooperating teacher.

FIRST DAY DISASTER

I took over Ms. Redding's classes the following Monday, and the first thing I remember is hearing the bell ring and then seeing a student come in the room and start walking on the tops of the desks to get to his seat.

"Don't climb on the furniture," I told him. "Come on, man. You're in seventh grade, you know better than that."

He sat down, and I went back to looking over my seating chart. Seating charts were the key to classroom management. Calling a student by his or her first name was extremely important and helped build a personal connection between the teacher and student. Kids were human just like everybody else; they enjoyed hearing their names.

There were two dozen students in the class. My chart was based on the seating arrangement Ms. Redding had already established—six rows of five desks. The majority of the students didn't have to sit in new seats; they just needed to keep the ones they'd been using the week I got there. Not all kids sat in the same seats every day, but they would now. I wasn't prepared to play musical chairs. I'd never learn their names that way.

The period was 40 minutes long. Getting the students quiet and seated in their assigned desks took 15 minutes—over one-third of the class. Several students complained about their new seat. They protested that it was too close to the front or next to someone they didn't like or that the desk was too big or too small for their liking. I told them to stop bellyaching and suck it up, making no attempt to compromise or be diplomatic. It was my way or the highway; that was my philosophy. If they didn't like it, too bad. This approach was a mistake from the start. It did nothing but provoke the kids and make them standoffish.

But I didn't know any better. I just wanted to crack the whip, like Ms. Donavan did. Lay down the law so there could be order and control.

After I went through the seating chart, I went into my rules and expectations. I talked about respect and common courtesy and how if someone wanted to make a comment or ask a question, he or she needed to raise his or her hand. I also explained that it was important for only one person to speak at a time. When I was talking, everyone was listening. When a fellow student was talking, everyone was listening. Ironically, kids were turned around in their desks and talking to their neighbors as I gave this lecture. It was the first period of my first day teaching Ms. Redding's kids, and I could see I was already losing half the class.

"Excuse me!" I shouted. "I need everyone facing forward so I can explain some important rules to you."

"Man, you is draw'n," a boy in the front said and rolled his eyes. "Draw'n" was an urban term that meant acting stupid or foolish. When someone did something that you didn't like or approve of, that person was "draw'n."

"What's your name?" I said to the student; although, I knew his name because I had the seating chart in my hand. I was doing this for effect, to set an example.

The student ignored me.

"Excuse me, you—what's your name?" I walked over to the student's desk and stood next to him.

"Man," the boy said, "you need to get outta my *face*."

I told him to step out into the hallway so I could have a word with him. He didn't move, so I stayed by his desk. Finally, he jumped up and stormed out of the classroom.

"Hold on a moment," I told the rest of the class and went into the hall to speak to the boy. When I got out there, he was leaning against a row of lockers and pouting, hands in his pockets, staring down at the floor.

"What's with the attitude?" I asked him. I was calm and making an effort to be understanding.

"Man, you draw'n," he said, not looking at me.

"How am I draw'n?"

"Cause you're pickin' on me."

"I'm not picking on you," I told him. "You're being disrespectful. You're talking and making comments while I'm trying to teach."

"The whole class is talkin'," he said. "You didn't say nothin' to nobody else."

"The whole class *isn't* talking," I told him.

"Yes they *is*."

"No they're not. But even if they *were*, that's none of your business. You need to worry about yourself and no one else, understand?"

The boy didn't say anything.

"From now on, I need you to face forward and pay attention to what I'm saying. No cocky comments under your breath, okay?"

"Man, whatever. Can I go back inside now?"

"Yes, but I want you to think about what I said. I'm very serious about this."

I followed the boy into the classroom. Ms. Redding was at the front of the room, keeping the students from going completely bananas. When I came back in, she went back to her desk and sat down.

The period was half over, and the students hadn't even opened a book yet.

MY SUPERVISOR'S SAGE ADVICE

Interestingly, as I struggled to control Ms. Redding's classes, I received no real tips or advice from my university student-teaching supervisor, Dr. Tanner. Outside of telling me to "be more assertive" when it came to discipline, the only thing my supervisor seemed to care about was that I wasn't adequately completing my paperwork. In addition to writing incredibly detailed lesson plans, student-teachers under Dr. Tanner were required to keep daily anecdotal records on actual students, write a 30-page instructional unit that stemmed from the current curriculum being taught at the co-op school, and compile a 75-page "resource portfolio" that contained genuine items from schools, such as sample hall passes, absent notes, report cards, pink slips, and so forth. Student-teachers were also required to put up a fancy academic-themed bulletin board in each building they worked in, take a picture of this, and place it in the portfolio.

The lesson plans themselves took hours to complete. They were based on the Madeline Hunter Model, which had the following categories: objectives (what the students should be able to do or understand as a result of the lesson), standards (the levels of expectations the teacher had for the students and how they would be held accountable for learning the material), anticipatory set (the "hook" to grab the students' attention and set a framework for ideas to follow), teaching process (the method of delivering instruction, including modeling and checking for understanding), guided practice (the teacher-supervised activity that allowed students to demonstrate their grasp of the new material), closure (actions that brought a lesson to a conclusion and reiterated major points), independent practice (homework or group work that reinforced content), materials (the list of items needed to teach the lesson), and duration (the amount of time needed to complete the lesson).

This was the basic template for our lesson plans, and every day we taught, we needed one. Because I taught both seventh and eighth grade English, I needed *two* a day—one for each subject. One day's plan was a page long, multiplied by two subjects equaled two pages. I taught 12 full weeks in all (the first week at each placement I only observed), so that came to a total of 60 days in the classroom or 120 pages of lesson plans. These plans were stored in a three-ring binder along with the daily anecdotal records I was required to keep on two students at each school with "behavioral problems."

Right from the start, Dr. Tanner insisted my plans weren't thorough enough. Some lacked details and didn't come to one full page. She also took issue with the verbs I chose in my objectives, like that fact that I wrote "identify" instead of "analyze," or "understand" instead of "comprehend." Today, after 14 years in the classroom, I still don't see why so much time is wasted on the verbiage of objectives.

Dr. Tanner's first formal observation of me took place in February back at Conwell and, for the most part, it went pretty well. I did a lesson on Jack London's short story "To Build a Fire," which came right out of the students' literature textbooks. I opened by having the students complete the following journal entry: "Describe a time in your life when you were freezing cold. Where were you? What were you wearing? How long was it until you were able to warm yourself up?"

After the students were finished writing, we shared our stories. I went first, telling about the time I went camping during my sophomore year in college in the middle of February and how the unseasonably warm temperature of 48 degrees suddenly fell to 25 degrees after midnight. I explained how it had rained all night and how all my gear got soaking wet and how I felt my sleeping bag icing up as I lay in it. I also told them that if I didn't do something, I would have probably died of hypothermia or at the very least had to get my legs amputated.

"So what'd you *do*?" a boy in the back of the room asked me.

"I had to wake up my friend and get the keys to his jeep."

"Then what happened?"

"I went inside and turned on the heat," I told them. "It took about an hour to warm up, and everything turned out fine."

After the journal, I had the students open their texts and make predictions about "To Build a Fire." I was very impressed with their responses as well as their enthusiasm. Once we got reading the story, Ms. Donavan took over so Dr. Tanner, who'd been observing me for the last 15 minutes, could pull me out in the hallway and have a short conference. Dr. Tanner told me that she thought I'd delivered "a solid nuts-and-bolts lesson." She said she liked the journal topic and the pre-reading strategies, and she thought things flowed well. She also said she'd spoken to Ms. Donavan about my teaching and that Ms. Donavan gave me a good report and noted that "I was very good with the kids."

Of course, Dr. Tanner pointed out, my lesson plans were a bit thin and my verbs were wrong. She took my binder from me, where I stored my plans, and began marking it up with a red pen. She wrote things like "more detail" and "flesh this out," and she even dotted some of my *i*'s and crossed some of my *t*'s. She gave the binder back to me and told me to work on it and to make sure I kept up with my anecdotal records on two problem students. Before she left, she pointed at my chin and noted that I had the beginnings of a blond beard growing there. She wanted to know: *Did I think this was professional? Would future principals want to hire me with this?* She left it up to me to decide. Then she left. This would be the last of any meaningful feedback I'd get from her for the rest of the semester.

FOUR
Teaching the Teachers

Over the past decade, teacher training has been the subject of much discussion. Critics of schoolteachers suggest their ineffectiveness is the direct result of inadequate teacher colleges and university education departments. Attacks on these institutions have been constant. Walter E. Williams, the John M. Olin Distinguished Professor of Economics at George Mason University, writes that if America truly wanted to improve public education, they'd shut down schools of education. "Schools of education, either graduate or undergraduate, represent the academic slums of any university," he says in a 2001 article. "They're home to students who have the lowest academic achievement test scores, be they the SAT, GRE, ACT, MCAT or LSAT. They're also home to professors with the lowest academic respect."[1]

Rita Kramer, distinguished author and social critic, writes in *Ed School Follies: The Miseducation of America's Teachers*, "We will never improve schooling . . . until we improve teacher education. What we have today are teacher-producing factories that process material from the bottom of the heap and turn out models that perform, but not well enough."[2]

Although supporters of teacher colleges may claim differently, a number of researchers, scholars, and education writers argue that, as a whole, schools of education are "cash cows" and stress quantity over quality. They also suggest education school admission standards are too low, their curriculum is inconsistent, and in general, they are teaching the wrong things to America's future educators.

Chapter 4

THE LEVINE REPORT

In 2006, Arthur Levine, former president of Teachers College at Columbia University, authored a report about the state of teacher training in America called *Educating School Teachers*. The report, considered one of the most comprehensive studies of education schools of the new millennium, is very frank in its findings. After a thorough survey of education school deans and faculty, teacher college graduates and alumni, and K–12 principals, Levine comes to the conclusion that "current teacher education programs are largely ill equipped to prepare current and future teachers for new realities."[3] In other words, Levine surmises, America's education schools can't keep up with our rapidly changing nation and the student body within it.

The fact that teachers graduate schools with instructional certificates yet enter classrooms unprepared for the job is not surprising. I myself was unprepared my first year teaching, and my experience was hardly an exception. Over my 14-year career in education, I've met at least a dozen new teachers who were completely overwhelmed their first year in the classroom. The majority of them never made it through the year, quitting out of frustration and sometimes finding a whole new line of work.

Discipline and classroom management was usually the primary reason for their failure. Generating lessons and new materials was also part of the problem. Most of the time, their instruction was mediocre at best. The few that made it through their rookie year learned on the job, figuring out the tricks of the trade through trial and error. Somehow they managed to survive all the things they didn't learn in college: dealing with fights, foul language, disengaged parents, students with behavioral and emotional problems, incompetent administrators, lack of resources and materials, and so forth.

Those that made it through their rookie years were still not proficient instructors right off. For some, like me, it took *years* to become a skilled educator. We cut our teeth on our students. Like comedians developing an act, we went out on stage in front of our students with our material and hoped it connected. And like comedians, it took class after class, day after day, month after month to generate something foolproof and workable. Of course, as teachers we were not trying to piecemeal together simply one 45-minute act to use for an entire year. We were trying to put together several 45-minute acts *per* day, new ones *every* day, for an entire year. Our education training, especially our methods courses, didn't appear to go far or deep enough.

According to the Levine report, principals were the most critical of education schools. "Only 40 percent on average thought schools of education were doing very or moderately well" when it came to preparing teachers.[4] This rating was based on 11 competencies, including how well teachers were taught to manage their classrooms; how well they were taught to assess student performance and utilize different pedagogical approaches; how prepared they were to address the needs of students with disabilities, limited English language proficiency, and diverse cultural backgrounds; and how well they mastered their subject matter.

One might assume the ratings were so low because no teacher school could possibly teach all of these skills to its graduates before they take a job. In fact, this would be the argument of those who believe that teaching is a craft as opposed to a profession; it's a practice that is learned on the job. However, when the heads of America's schools of education were asked in the Levine report if education schools were the best place to train teachers in these competencies, the overwhelming majority said that they were.

A GAP BETWEEN THEORY AND PRACTICE

Over the years, a major complaint I've heard from first-year teachers is that too much of what professors teach in college lacks practicality. In other words, the theories espoused in academia don't translate well in K–12 classrooms.

This was one of my biggest issues during student teaching. I remember paging through my college texts and the notes I'd taken during lectures and thinking, "Wow, I don't think this is going to fly at all." Much of the time it *didn't*. The big problem was getting the theory—things like constructivism, differentiated instruction, and interdisciplinary education—and building workable lessons out of it. The majority of my college professors never told me how to do *that*. Making the leap from the abstract to the concrete was apparently up to me.

The theory I *did* learn didn't cover half the crises I faced in the classroom. I never learned how to handle a parent who had absolutely no interest in her child's schooling. I never learned how to teach a class when half the students walked through the door without a notebook or a writing utensil. I never learned how to hold the attention of a 14-year-old boy who was high on marijuana. I never learned how to pick and choose my battles during the day so I didn't burn out by 10:30 in the morning. I never learned how to cultivate the proper sense of humor so when the class clown imitated the way I walked, I didn't blow my stack like a madman. I never learned how to deal with a student who refused to surrender his cell phone.

The instructional strategies I was taught in my college "methods" classes were also limited. A number of these methods—like the classic KWL reading strategy, think-pair-share, story mapping, and the use of anticipation guides to spark student interest—worked well for a while, but after a few weeks, they became repetitive. Other instructional methods I learned in college, such as "role-playing," often backfired. I'd begin them with enthusiasm, but after five minutes, it became clear the attitudes and the attention spans of my students were not conducive to the activity.

I'll never forget the time I tried a role-playing activity, which was all the rage in my methods courses as an undergraduate, with the students in Ms. Redding's English classes at Stewart. We were reading "The Most Dangerous Game" by Richard Connell, and I wanted students to not only comprehend the plot but also to analyze the traits of the two main characters, Rainsford and General Zaroff. I also wanted them to understand the mentality of the "hunter versus the hunted." I split the class of 28 eighth graders into 14 groups of two and had each group first create an original dialogue between Rainsford and Zaroff and prepare to read it aloud to the class, playing the role of each character. I even brought in some props—a phony plastic rifle (being that the story centered on hunting) and a fake mustache.

The first pair of students took the floor. For the first 30 seconds or so, the two read their lines back and forth, but soon they were off task, goofing with the rifle and putting the mustache on every which way. The rest of the class joined in, making inappropriate comments and talking out of turn. I stopped the lesson several times to re-explain my classroom rules, but the goofing still continued. Only three groups managed to go through their dialogues before the activity became unmanageable and I had to revert back to simply reading aloud from the book.

Curiously, the role-playing activity looked good on paper. The overall lesson incorporated multiple learning styles, was interdisciplinary, and figured to be a great way to keep students interested. However, the skills needed to effectively manage this kind of instruction were extensive, especially in an urban setting with special needs children. At the time, I didn't possess these skills. Some might say they were unteachable in an isolated college classroom setting. Others might argue they *were* teachable but simply not adequately addressed by my education professors.

LACK OF TEACHING EXPERIENCE

Another criticism of teacher colleges is that too many education professors are disconnected from the realities of K–12 classrooms. "Teacher educators as a group tend to discourage scientific research on the effectiveness and effects of the pedagogical theories and practices that they promote in coursework for aspiring or practicing teachers and administrators," writes Sandra Stotsky, professor, researcher, and former senior associate commissioner at the Massachusetts Department of Education.[5]

Stotsky's remarks are curious, if not controversial. Those who believe teacher educators discourage scientific research on the effectiveness of their theories might want to know *why*. One might argue this problem stems from the fact that many don't actually have to *use* the strategies they teach in real K–12 classrooms. In other words, some teacher educators are so isolated from America's public school system that there is no urgency for them to keep the instructional strategies they teach grounded and practical.

Students and alumni surveyed in the Levine report complained that the courses taught by their education professors were "out of date, more theoretical than practical, and thin in content."[6] Alumni in the report explained that assignments given by out-of-touch professors were useless: "It was all hypothetical. Prepare a lesson and remember you have four special needs students in class. That's real easy if you are pretending, but try it in a real class-room."[7]

A lack of adequate time in a K–12 public school classroom can also affect a professor's *teaching*. When I look back on my experiences in both undergraduate and graduate school, my professors were, for the most part, well prepared. Classroom environment was a nonissue (college students are mature adults paying a substantial amount of money to get an education); although, the environments of some of the classes in which my professors taught were lifeless and clinical.

Instruction, on the other hand, was at times lacking. Few of my professors differentiated instruction to fit various learning styles, and not enough used a variety of questioning and discussion techniques. Too many of them lectured—chalk and talk—and failed to fully engage students in learning. They simply tried to deposit knowledge into our brains rather than allowing us to arrive at the new information ourselves. In addition, some couldn't effectively communicate with students and were inflexible.

Once, as an undergraduate, I was taking an education course on creating student assessments. Basically, it was a course that taught us how to create valid and reliable tests to measure students with diverse learning and testing styles.

"Good teachers shouldn't simply give written tests and quizzes," the professor explained, "but should also provide various hands-on projects and oral reports." The basis of the course was Bloom's taxonomy of higher-order questioning.

The course turned out a little differently from what I had expected. For starters, the textbook the professor assigned was ancient—from the late 1970s. It was horribly dry and filled with tedious, long-winded theory on the principles of assessment. A single chapter took hours to struggle though. However, it was well known around campus that book knowledge in this particular course was secondary. The way to get an A in this professor's class was to score extra points on the two bonus quizzes she gave randomly during the semester. The bonus quizzes were worth a total of 50 extra points (the small one was 10 points, and the big one was 40). These were based on notes from classroom lectures and, if applied, could bring your overall grade from a C to an A. You had to be in class that day to take the bonus quiz (there were no make-ups because it was a "bonus"), and this was apparently the professor's attempt to keep cutting to a minimum.

Most students had a C average because, aside from constructing one sample test using all six levels of Bloom's Taxonomy, our grade was based primarily on the weekly multiple choice quizzes that came straight from the teacher's edition of the ancient textbook. The irony was so thick you could choke on it: the professor teaching us how to design diverse student assessments wasn't using a diverse system of assessment herself.

IMPROVEMENTS AND REFORM

In October of 2009, U.S. Education Secretary Arne Duncan gave a speech at the University of Virginia to an audience of aspiring teachers from the Curry School of Education. Titled "A Call to Teaching," the speech attempted to motivate students into becoming the kind of educators America's children so badly needed and deserved. The speech also bluntly criticized schools of education. Duncan remarked:

> In far too many universities, education schools are the neglected stepchild. Too often they don't attract the best students or faculty. The programs are heavy on educational theory—and light on developing core area knowledge and clinical training under the supervision of master teachers. Generally, not enough attention is paid to what works to boost student learning—and student teachers are not trained in how to use data to improve their instruction and drive a cycle of continuous improvement for their students. Many ed. schools do relatively little to prepare students for the rigor of teaching in high-poverty and high-need schools.[8]

Sharon P. Robinson, president and CEO of the American Association of Colleges for Teacher Education (AACTE), received Duncan's comments with mixed emotions. In an official response headlined "Looking for Leadership with a Vision of the Future," Robinson answers Duncan's remarks by posting a letter on AACTE's website: "I read with disappointment Secretary Duncan's speech at the University of Virginia on October 9. While I applaud the Administration's recognition of teaching as an honorable profession, I am sorry the focus of the speech was, once again, on shopworn criticisms of educator preparation programs."[9]

Robinson goes on to explain that there were many colleges of education that had successfully implemented reforms. She notes many had increased the rigor of content preparation; that many focused on teaching educators to use student assessment data to aid their instruction; that

FIVE
First Year

In June of 1995, not even a month after I graduated college with a BS in secondary education, I applied for a teaching position with the Philadelphia School District. The application process involved taking the district's official teacher of English test—a written exam combined with an interview and mini teaching lesson—which I passed. Later that summer, I received a letter in the mail that explained I had been officially placed on a waiting list with nearly 100 other English teachers and that I would be notified when district administrators got to my name.

Two years later, after working a half-dozen menial jobs, which included a nine-month stint as an advertising agency assistant in Baltimore, Maryland, the Philadelphia School District finally called me up for service. In August of 1997, I was officially invited by the district to report to their central office building at 21st and Arch streets to review their English teacher vacancy list and select a school. After I signed an agreement to teach at Lincoln High School in Northeast Philadelphia, I was informed later that week by the principal's secretary that I was being assigned not to Lincoln's main campus but to an off-campus called Swenson Skills Center.

In 1997, Swenson was a school in transition. For nearly 20 years, Swenson was strictly a vocational school, offering programs in carpentry, plumbing, cosmetology, horticulture, and a dozen other skill-based trades. Students interested in pursuing a career in one of these vocations would alternate time between their neighborhood school and Swenson, usually spending a half-day in each. For the most part, this system worked. Students learned a hands-on skill that they could take into the real word and earn a decent living.

Then in the early 1990s, the direction of vocational education began to change in Philadelphia. School reformers believed sending students to vocational schools was creating a dual-class system—a system that was giving "vo-tech" students an inferior education. To end the stigma associated with trade schools, Philadelphia School District leaders began pushing academics over trades. As a result, many of the city's vocational schools were restructured to include core academic subjects—English, math, science, social studies, and the like. This way, students would have everything they needed in one building, and vo-tech students would get the kind of "rigorous" educations district officials believed they needed to succeed.

In the fall of 1993, Swenson accepted its first full-time freshman class. Because Swenson now contained all the subjects needed for students to graduate in the state of Pennsylvania, these freshmen no longer divided their time between Swenson and their neighborhood school; Swenson *was* their school. To open up academic classes, shops had to close. Students interested in vocational programs no longer offered at Swenson were forced to settle for trades that were their second or third choices.

This transition took a toll on the school. When shops started to close at Swenson, enrollment dropped, and student interest waned. Although there were many intelligent, dedicated students who went to Swenson in the late 1990s, some students found themselves there by default. Because it had neither a broad academic curriculum that appealed to college-bound students nor the wide variety of vocational programs it once offered, kids were often sent to Swenson who had nowhere else to go— who'd been kicked out of their neighborhood schools for behavioral or discipline issues. Fortunately, the school did not remain in this condition for long. Swenson Skills Center would eventually become Swenson Arts and Technology High School in 2000 and undergo a complete transformation.

I showed up at Swenson that first Tuesday morning in September of 1997 at 8:00 a.m. and was given the only remaining English roster—four classes of freshman and one class of sophomores. Besides my roster, I was given no other materials, no ninth- or tenth-grade English curriculum, no scope or sequence guide. I wasn't even provided with the basic supplies for my classroom, like chalk and erasers, folders, pens and paper, or any other stationery needed to get started in the classroom.

"Buy it at Staples," I was told by one of the veteran teachers. This was a theme I would learn soon enough. To do things right in the Philadelphia School District in 1997, teachers needed to dip into their own pockets.

Sally Myers, the Swenson teacher who was supposed to be serving as my mentor and helping me get set up in my classroom, was nowhere to be found. She had shaken my hand earlier that morning and said, "Hello, Christopher, I'm Sally Myers. I'll be serving as your mentor this year," but then she disappeared into the woodwork for the rest of the day; I didn't see her again for three months.

I found my way to my room and tried to scrounge together materials. I managed to hunt down a set of worn ninth-grade literature texts from a makeshift bookroom. No one in the English department could point me in the direction of 10th-grade texts, however. I'd searched the school from top to bottom, but there were no books to be found.

I sat in my empty classroom, walls barren, shelves empty, and paged through the ninth-grade literature book at my desk. I tried to formulate some plan of attack for the year, some way to approach teaching both ninth- and tenth-grade English. The reality was, I hadn't stepped inside a classroom in almost two years, and anything left over from student teaching was long gone. It was time to start from scratch again, to rebuild an arsenal of activities to educate my students. I didn't have much to work with, but I'd have to make do.

I opened my leather shoulder bag, took out a notepad, and began working out my lessons.

CULTURE SHOCK

Teaching at Swenson was a culture shock. I went to 12 years of Catholic school, and although I had a diverse group of friends who often hung out in the city, I was more accustomed to life in the suburbs. My peers and I were refined and came from stable two-parent families. In school, we all wore uniforms—slacks, shoes, shirt, tie, school sweater. We were, for the most part, clean-cut and neatly kempt (hair had to be short and off the collar), respectful, courteous, and studious. We did our fair share of rule breaking and screwing around, but we never strayed too far from the path.

Swenson students, who were at the time 60 percent white, 30 percent black, and 10 percent Hispanic, were different. They were harder, more jaded. They had that neighborhood edge to them. One morning in early September, I remember crossing the school parking lot on my way into the building and seeing a confrontation between two seniors. The one kid was driving his car with his girlfriend in the passenger seat, and the other kid had mistakenly walked out in front of the car and banged into the hood. The kid driving started cursing at him.

"You touch my car I'll beat your fuckin' face!" he shouted and jumped out. He was wearing a "wife beater"—one of those tank-top T-shirts Robert De Niro wore in *Raging Bull*. The other kid, who was smaller, apologized and backed away. I watched the incident, my adrenaline pumping, and felt out of my element.

The upper-grade Swenson girls also had an edge to them. Some were just as hard as the boys, ready to throw a punch at the drop of a hat. They wore tons of makeup and jewelry, smoked Marlboro Lights, and dressed in clothing that was too tight and too low cut. This made many of them look my age, in their early 20s, and I was always uneasy around them; I remember how floored I was when I saw a *pregnant girl* in my last-period 10th-grade English class.

In light of this, I was glad to be teaching mostly freshman.

Surprisingly, my teaching career at Swenson started off rather smoothly. During the whole first week of classes, the ninth graders were basically quiet and kept to themselves, following my classroom rules and just trying to survive high school in a brand new building. We covered the basics of writing a five-paragraph persuasive essay, a unit I worked on at home with my father, who was teaching English and social studies at the business annex of John Bartram High School in Southwest Philadelphia.

With my father as my unofficial mentor, I designed my first week's lesson. That Monday, I went over the writing process from top to bottom with all my English classes. I taught them to brainstorm for ideas, to narrow these ideas down to a single topic, to develop a thesis and supporting arguments for the topic, to write out the first draft in five-paragraph form, to revise the first draft through peer editing, and to rewrite a final copy. This took the whole first week. The students were engaged and cooperated as well as could be expected.

The second week, I did a short story called "Initiation" by Sylvia Plath. It was about the hazing of a high-school girl who is being initiated into a teenage social club. I was excited by the story because I could relate to it; only five years earlier, I was initiated into the Pi Kappa chapter of the Zeta Psi fraternity at Bloomsburg University. The hazing during pledging was intense, and some of these scars were still fresh. I figured I could take this energy and my experiences and incorporate them into my lesson to make it interesting.

As a hook to get the kid's attention, I brought in my actual fraternity paddle and showed it to the class. The paddle was a foot and a half long, cut by yours truly from a pine two-by-four during the spring of 1992. It was lacquered dark brown and had 14 strips of athletic tape on each side. On each strip of tape was the signature of every fraternity brother I had pledged under. The signatures were done in pen and colored markers. Earning the signatures sometimes involved chugging a full beer or cleaning out somebody's car or, in rare cases, eating something disgusting, like a whole onion—skin included. There was other writing on my paddle besides the signatures, like: "smoke more weed," or "fuck fat chicks," or "do beer bongs." Because of this, I couldn't pass the paddle around for the students to look at it individually; I didn't want them to get a glimpse of my sordid past. Instead, I held it up in the front of the room and let them admire it from afar.

Right away, there were protests. They wanted to *hold* the paddle, turn it over in their hot little hands.

"Sorry," I told them. "I can't pass it around."

"Why not?"
"Because there's bad words on it."
"Curses?"
"Yep."
So what? They insisted. *We've heard curse words before.*

It wasn't an option. I put the paddle away in my desk and moved forward with the lesson.

The third week, I covered the short stories "The Tunnel" and "The Sniper." It was around this time that full-time teaching, and all its pressures and responsibilities, started to catch up to me. I was not only feeling physically drained but was struggling to generate fresh material that could keep the attention of the freshmen and channel their energy. My lessons were already starting to become mundane. Kids were complaining that they were tired of doing the same "stupid" activities. It was also around this time that the freshmen were becoming more comfortable with each other and with the school. Their timidity was turning to curiosity, and they started testing the waters. They began challenging my classroom rules and authority. Soon their unruliness was in full swing, a sign that our honeymoon period was ending.

By Thanksgiving, I was losing the students. To them, my voice became a droning monotone that they just wanted to turn off like a static-filled radio station. At the time, I was unable to adapt my lessons or teaching style; I was too inexperienced. I raised my voice and argued with my students, competing with them and trying to get in the last word. Tempers flared, and some students came to resent me.

The discipline office at the time gave me little support. One of the reasons was because I wrote too many pink slips. Pink slips were supposed to be a last resort, a measure taken by teachers when they'd exhausted all other options. There was a protocol to follow before writing a pink slip: a one-on-one conference with the child, a detention, a phone call home. If there was still a problem at this point, the teacher might consider writing a pink slip. The only way teachers could circumvent this system was if the initial offense was a "serious incident." Teachers who inundated the discipline office with pink slips for questionable offenses were very quickly put on the *pay-no-mind list*.

By December, I found myself at the top of this list. It was clear the discipline office felt that my classroom management was less than exemplary and that most of the problems I was experiencing were my own fault, brought on by inexperience. Why should the discipline office waste its limited resources on a teacher who simply couldn't control his class?

This was only half true, however. There were two separate "serious incidents" that I felt were not handled appropriately. Once that spring, I got into a confrontation with one of my students in the hallway. After a brief exchange of words, the student challenged me to a fight. I didn't back off. Standing nose-to-nose, the student said, "Paslay, I'll *kick your fuckin' ass*."

I was so angry, I was shaking. I wrote-up the incident on a pink slip, explaining that I was threatened and verbally assaulted by a student. To my outrage, after the discipline office made a perfunctory effort to find the student in the building but couldn't, nothing was done. No suspension or any follow-up was made.

Another time, while I was teaching one afternoon, a student asked to go to the bathroom. There was only 10 minutes left in class and my rule was no hall passes the first or last 15 minutes of the period. I told the student to wait until the end of class, but he refused. He got up to leave, and I went over to the door to stop him.

"You have to wait for the bell," I told him and made the rookie mistake of blocking the doorway with my arm.

"Man, I gotta *piss*," he told me and shoved my arm out of the way. My blood boiled in my veins. I followed him down the hall, shouting at him. I explained that this was assault, that he was in serious trouble, that chances were he was going to be arrested. I called for school security, and when an officer came, the two of us escorted the boy to discipline. When I got to the dean's office, I erupted. I recounted the situation, and as I did, the boy who'd shoved my arm just rolled his eyes and shrugged.

I returned to my classroom right as the bell rang. The kids flooded out of the room in a stampede, and I had to step aside to let them through the door. When I finally got inside my room, I found that it had been trashed: during my five-minute absence, some wise guy had turned on the sink in the corner, and water was gushing out of the spigot; they had taken apart my oscillating fan, and now it was blowing without a cage on the front; they had turned on my Channel One television and put the volume up to maximum so now it was making a loud hissing sound as snow flashed on the screen.

I was on the verge of losing it. I cleaned up my room to get ready for the next class.

Later that week, I found out what happened to the boy who pushed my arm: he was given two detentions by the discipline office.

SIX
School Leaders and Supports

According to a June 2007 policy brief issued by the National Commission on Teaching and America's Future (NCTAF) titled "The High Cost of Teacher Turnover," public-school teacher turnover is costing America over 7 billion dollars a year. Teacher attrition has grown by 50 percent in the past two decades. Nationally, the teacher turnover rate has risen to 16.8 percent, and in some districts, the teacher dropout rate is higher than the student dropout rate.[1]

The NCTAF policy brief sums up the situation this way:

> Until we recognize that we have a retention problem we will continue to engage in a costly annual recruitment and hiring cycle, pouring more and more teachers into our nation's classrooms only to lose them at a faster and faster rate. This will continue to drain our public tax dollars, it will undermine teaching quality, and it will most certainly hinder our ability to close student achievement gaps.[2]

Teacher turnover is expensive. When a teacher retires, resigns, or transfers from services, a school must use a portion of its budget to find a replacement. This cost involves advertising, recruiting, and training a new hire to fill the vacant position. It was estimated by NCTAF in 2007 that, in Chicago, every teacher who quit his or her job cost the system $17,872; annually, teacher turnover costs Chicago $86 million. In Los Angeles, it costs $94 million. In New York, $115 million.[3]

Teacher retention, although a national problem, is particularly troubling in large, urban school districts; in big cities, according to 2007 statistics, one in five drops out every year.[4] In the Philadelphia School District, of the 919 new teachers hired during the 1999–2000 school year, only 30 percent remained in the district after six years.[5]

Besides its high costs, teacher turnover is preventing the equal distribution of quality teachers in all classrooms. High-poverty, low-performing schools tend to have the least-experienced teachers and those with the poorest credentials. In a report titled *The Quest for Quality: Recruiting and Retaining Teachers in Philadelphia*, Research for Action, a Philadelphia nonprofit education-research organization, found that in Philadelphia during the 2003–04 school year, 56 percent of all new middle school teachers had no certification.[6] During that same year, public schools that had 90 percent of the student body below the poverty level had staffs where 25 percent of the teachers had one year or less experience in the classroom.[7]

There are several reasons behind this high turnover and unequal distribution of teachers. One problem is the lack of supports new teachers receive. In their Quest for Quality study, Research for Action found that many of Philadelphia's new teachers lacked basic supports during their first week on the job. During the 2002–2003 school year, only 32 percent of the 366 teachers surveyed said they received a curriculum scope and sequence, 64 percent said they were given a staff handbook, 50 percent said they were told the name of their union representative, and only 73 percent were given a mailbox.[8]

In defense of the Philadelphia School District, conditions have been steadily improving since 2000. Paul Vallas, who became CEO of city schools in 2002, standardized district curriculum and spent millions on upgrading materials and books. An emphasis was also placed on teacher recruitment and retention, and more teachers were placed in hard-to-staff schools. In addition, building conditions were improved, and new schools were erected. The High School of the Future—the district's first "paperless" school built in partnership with Microsoft—opened its doors in West Philadelphia in 2006 after three years of careful planning and construction.

District progress continued under the new leadership of Superintendent Dr. Arlene Ackerman in 2008, who was named top urban school leader in the United States by the Council of Great City Schools in October of 2010.[9] Under her Imagine 2014 school reform plan, which was composed using input from teachers, students, parents, and the entire Philadelphia education community, 150 counselors were added to middle schools and high schools, class sizes were lowered in the early grades, and summer programs were expanded.

Supports directly aimed at assisting teachers at a classroom level also increased. Professional Development Centers were opened to help staff take courses customized to their specific interests and needs, and first-year teacher supports—such as mentoring and induction programs—were strengthened. Most notably, the Office of Teacher Affairs was opened under Dr. Ackerman. "The mission of the Office of Teacher Affairs," according to the district's website, "is to serve as a hub to support, inform, and act as a resource for teachers from hiring to retirement. A goal of this office is to make certain all teachers can experience a timely response to their specific needs."[10]

Districts, such as Philadelphia's, should be applauded for their efforts to improve teacher supports. However, there is still plenty of work to be done to address both the problem of teacher retention as well as teacher equity.

SCHOOL SAFETY

As with any profession, teachers need to feel safe in order to do their jobs properly. Unfortunately, too many schools in America are plagued by crime and violence. In the 2007–2008 school year, there were nearly 15,000 criminal incidents reported in Philadelphia public schools.[11] According to data published in the *Philadelphia Inquirer*, 1,728 students assaulted teachers, 479 weapons were discovered inside elementary and middle school hallways and classrooms, and 357 weapons were found in high schools.[12]

Tragically, almost half of the most serious cases were not reported to police. *Inquirer* reporter Kristen Graham writes that "the most serious offenders—including those who assaulted teachers—were neither expelled nor transferred to alternative education." She also adds: "Just 24 percent of the 1,728 students who assaulted teachers were removed from regular education classrooms, and only 30 percent of them were charged by police."[13]

In fact, from 2006 to 2008, not a single student was expelled from the Philadelphia School District.[14] Although it may be hard for those outside urban education to comprehend, there are reasons why school officials choose not to remove students from the system. One big deterrent is money. Compulsory education laws in most states dictate that if a district opts to remove a student from one of its schools, then it's the district's responsibility to find an alternative placement for that child. This can be time consuming and costly and drain the already thin resources of large urban districts.

Another deterrent is the existence of special education laws. The Individuals with Disabilities Education Act (IDEA) has several statutory provisions that in some cases literally make it illegal for schools to expel students. One is called "least-restrictive environment," and the other is a "stay-put" provision for pending discipline cases. For the most part, these laws guarantee that children with disabilities—whether behavioral or instructional—have the right to an education in an environment where they can interact and socialize with nondisabled children and where they are least likely to be stigmatized. If counselors deem it appropriate, this environment is usually a regular-education classroom. Technically, a disabled child could become violent and confrontational and still be allowed to remain in a regular classroom if it is determined that the behavioral episode was a manifestation of his or her disability.[15] Lawsuits abound in the world of special education, which is why many school officials choose to keep the unruly child in the building rather than attempting to have him or her expelled.

On top of this, the No Child Left Behind law used both suspensions and expulsions to determine a school's Adequate Yearly Progress rating. This undoubtedly influenced school leaders' decisions when it came to keeping violent students in the classroom.

Fortunately, there are those fighting to change the status quo. During the 2008–2009 school year, Dr. Arlene Ackerman made school safety a priority. She adopted a "zero tolerance" policy for violence and helped to streamline the process for holding expulsion hearings. By May of 2009, the school district had voted on the expulsion of 33 students—12 of whom were permanently expelled, 13 who were temporarily expelled, and 8 who were allowed to remain in the system.[16]

Despite Ackerman's best efforts, however, crime and safety were still an issue in 2009. In June of that year, the *Philadelphia Inquirer* obtained a folder of reports detailing discipline incidents that occurred in Philadelphia city schools from June 1 thru 5. In an editorial headlined "Can't Learn in Bad Schools," the *Inquirer* writes:

> The incidents range from students bringing knives and guns to school, masturbating in class, going to school drunk, pulling down other students' pants, making death threats, punching a teacher in the face, stealing thousands of dollars worth of equipment, throwing an eraser at a teacher's head, and stuffing feces in bathroom sinks.[17]

The *Inquirer* editorial also mentions an incident where a teacher asked a student to stop eating food in class. When the student refused, the teacher tried to take the food and was then smacked in the face by the student. In another part of the city during that same week, the editorial noted, an elementary student grabbed a fire extinguisher from a hallway and began spraying a teacher in the face.[18]

To increase the retention rate of teachers in America and to help get a qualified teacher in every classroom, safety must become a bigger priority.

PERFORMANCE PAY

In 2009, President Obama's Race to the Top contest began offering billions of dollars in grants to lure public school districts across the country to experiment with performance pay. The logic was that offering bonuses for success in the classroom would increase the quality of instruction and motivate teachers to raise the bar and strive harder for excellence. To many politicians pushing for better schools, the idea seemed reasonable. Money talks, so do results. Why not have performance pay in every school?

In 2010, two notable studies on performance pay were released with the following conclusion: *performance pay had no effect on student achievement*. The first study, by Mathematica Policy Research, took place in Chicago and was published in May of 2010. Of the study, *Education Week* reporter Stephen Sawchuk writes:

> Preliminary results from schools taking part in a Chicago program containing performance-based compensation for teachers show no evidence that the program has boosted student achievement on math and reading tests, compared with a group of similar, nonparticipating schools, an analysis released last week concludes.[19]

A second study, which involved almost 300 middle school math teachers in Nashville, Tennessee and was released in September of 2010, revealed much of the same results. Of this study, *Education Week* reporter Sawchuk writes:

> The most rigorous study of performance-based teacher compensation ever conducted in the United States shows that a nationally watched bonus-pay system had no overall impact on student achievement—results released today that are certain to set off a firestorm of debate.[20]

Interestingly, a "firestorm of debate" didn't materialize, at least not immediately. In the weeks following the report's release, supporters of merit pay all but ignored the study, dismissing the findings as premature and too narrow. In fact, some education reformers held even *tighter* to the idea of using merit pay to boost student achievement. New Jersey governor Chris Christi, one week after the findings were made public, announced that he was going to indeed tie teacher pay to student achievement.[21]

Despite enthusiasm from politicians such as Christi, many of America's schoolteachers insist they are not motivated by merit pay. According to a 2010 report conducted by Scholastic and the Bill and Melinda Gates Foundation titled *Primary Sources: America's Teachers on America's Schools*, supportive leadership is listed by educators as the most important factor impacting teacher retention. Time given for teachers to collaborate is ranked second, followed by access to high-quality curriculum and a clean and safe building environment. Ranked ninth—dead last—was merit pay.[22]

Likewise, not many teachers felt monetary rewards for teacher performance would have a strong impact on student achievement. Of the 40,000 teachers surveyed in the study, 30 percent said that merit pay would have no impact at all, while 41 percent said it would only have a moderate impact.[23]

Still, supporters of performance pay insist it's a viable way to increase learning. Dom Giordano, a Philadelphia-based broadcaster and radio personality, wrote in a 2010 commentary for the *Philadelphia Daily News* that, "all signs point to the conclusion that teachers should join the real world and get paid based on performance."[24] Giordano's less-than-polite remarks are not only typical of the public's anti-teacher sentiment but also an example of how grossly misinformed the average person is on the workings of education (yes, I am well aware that back when dinosaurs roamed the earth, Mr. Giordano was a schoolteacher). Merit pay may indeed deserve further exploration, but to insinuate that teachers live in some fairytale world is preposterous. If teaching is so easy, if educators are taking free money, then why do so many quit every year? Why is teacher retention costing America seven billion dollars annually?

The fact remains that teaching *isn't* easy, that despite low test scores, nearly all teachers face enough daily challenges to earn their keep. This isn't to say school reformers should abandon performance pay, but the idea should be approached carefully and with the support and input of educators themselves.

CLASS SIZE

Does class size make a difference in student achievement? The answer to this question depends upon who you ask. According to the *State of Tennessee's Student/Teacher Achievement Ratio Project* (commonly known as the STAR report), class size is indeed significant. A well-known and trusted study on teacher-student ratios, the STAR report monitored the achievement of 7,000 students in kindergarten through third grade in nearly 100 schools across the state of Tennessee. The study took place over four years, from 1985 to 1989, and included 300 classrooms from urban, rural, and suburban districts.

The STAR report offers the following conclusion: "Each of the four years, small-class students in both reading and math (as well as in other SAT subtests) achieved significantly higher test scores than students in regular classes."[25] The report also notes that small classes benefited students from all racial and socioeconomic backgrounds and reduced grade retention.

The results of the STAR report and others like it were quickly embraced by the education community. Throughout the 1990s, efforts to reduce class sizes became the focus of many politicians and school reformers across the United States. President Bill Clinton and his education secretary, Richard Riley, led the charge.

"Reducing class size is one of the most important investments we can make in our children's future," said President Clinton. "Recent research confirms what parents have always known—children learn better in small classes with good teachers, and kids who start out in smaller classes do better right through their high school graduation."[26]

In 1999, the U.S. Department of Education launched its Class-Size Reduction Program, and Congress provided $1.2 billion for schools to hire new classroom teachers for the 1999–2000 school year to help improve the teacher-student ratio.[27] In September of 2000, a year after the program was in place, the federal government issued a first-year report on the program, deeming it a success.

The report notes that the program helped turn around failing schools in Washington, DC, and Columbus, Ohio; that it helped improve reading achievement in Maryland, Mississippi, and Pennsylvania; and that it helped improve individualized instruction and classroom management in Illinois and Virginia. In New York City, the program decreased disciplinary referrals in city schools, improved teacher morale, and led to higher levels of classroom participation by students.[28]

Most importantly, the program was applauded almost unanimously by teachers. According to the report, a teacher in West Middlesex, Pennsylvania, said:

> I had a good idea of each child's basic ability by the first week of school, because I had more time to spend with each child individually. I knew very early on who to watch for potential learning and behavior problems. . . . Each child also had more time to share his thoughts and ideas in both oral and written form. . . . There also were few behavior problems. . . . Since everything that we did this year took so much less time than usual, we were able to do so much more.[29]

However, not everyone was convinced spending billions of dollars to reduce class size was worth the money. In November of 2003, the peer-reviewed journal *Education Policy Analysis* published a report called *The Relationship between Exposure to Class Size Reduction and Student Achievement in California*. The study, conducted by the RAND Corporation, attempts to determine whether or not recent improvement in student achievement is a direct result of the federal government's Class-Size Reduction program. The study draws the following conclusion:

> The analyses show that scores at the elementary level have been rising at the same time that increasing percentages of students have been taught in reduced size classes. However, many other educational reforms were enacted during this period that might have contributed to the achievement gains, and it is impossible for us to determine how much the various factors may have influenced trends in overall student achievement.[30]

In other words, the RAND report on Class-Size Reduction (CSR) is inconclusive. In California, lowering class sizes *may* have been helping student achievement over time, but the RAND study could not test for cumulative effects of several years of exposure to CSR.

But this report was enough for those opposed to spending billions to cut class sizes. It was also good for helping George W. Bush change the direction of education in America. With a new president came a new agenda for America's schools, and this new agenda was more concerned with *outcomes* than it was with *processes*. No Child Left Behind, which held students to the highest standards of achievement in our nation's history, focused primarily on data and test scores. Basically, if student outcomes couldn't be measured on a standardized test, they weren't worth much.

Tragically, many of the benefits of lowering class sizes—benefits both acknowledged and embraced by President Clinton and his administration—were not able to be adequately measured by the reading and math tests prescribed by No Child Left Behind. Studies show lowering class size improves both teacher and student morale and enthusiasm, but morale and enthusiasm can't be tracked and tested. Cutting class size also improves discipline, school safety, teacher-student relationships, classroom management, individualized instruction, and student participation, but these aren't easily tracked by numbers and data.

So through the 2000s, the fight for reducing class size waned. In fact, politicians and reformers looking to balance budgets targeted class size as a way of saving money. *Why should we spend millions on cutting class sizes when the research shows that it doesn't have an effect on student achievement?* many argued, referencing the conclusions drawn by the RAND study. Dom Giordano, the Philadelphia radio personality and media celebrity, even names class size as one of education's "5 Big Lies" in a 2009 *Philadelphia Daily News* commentary, insisting the number of students in a classroom had no relevant bearing on learning, and yes, he cites the RAND study as his source of evidence.[31]

In October of 2010, Florida was fighting to *increase* class size by three students and to amend a 2002 law that kept class sizes in the state to 18 students in elementary school, 22 in middle school, and 25 in high school. Critics of Florida's attempt to change the class-size law claimed it was really about funding because a rule change could have saved the state up to $1 billion in class-size costs every year.[32]

There's no debating that reducing class size is expensive. Additional teachers and personnel cost money, and in a slow economy, money can be tight. However, the argument that class size has no real bearing on student achievement is a misnomer. Although it's true that good instruction trumps the size of a class, good instruction is not always possible with high numbers of students.

To see if class size has an impact on learning, you only need to ask yourself two fundamental questions: (1) *Does classroom management have an effect on learning?* It most certainly does. Any legitimate educator who's spent time in a classroom will tell you that you can't teach a class that you can't control. And (2) *Does class size have an effect on classroom management?* Without a doubt, it does. You can manage 15 students much more effectively than 30. There are fewer behavioral issues; there is a stronger teacher-to-student ratio; there is less time needed to produce and grade materials so there is more time to plan for instruction; when it comes to resources, such as computers and money for field trips, you can accommodate 15 much easier than 30; and the list goes on and on. These factors not only impact on learning but also on the teacher-student relationship and the closeness of the classroom environment.

Even in the cases where class size was reduced and student achievement did not increase, the problem most likely stemmed from *instruction* and the teacher's failure to adapt his or her teaching to the smaller group. As *Education Week* reporter Linda Jacobson wrote in February of 2001:

> Increasingly, both educators and some researchers say they are convinced that teachers, and what they do in smaller classes, are the real key to whether class-size reduction improves student achievement. Simply reducing the size of a class may not be enough. The real payoff appears to come when teachers shift their practices to take advantage of having fewer students.[33]

Class size has a very real impact on student learning in the 21st century. School reformers should do everything within reason to improve the teacher-student ratio within America's classrooms and provide teachers with the proper training to take advantage of these smaller numbers.

TREATING TEACHERS AS SPECIALISTS

In October of 2009, Education Secretary Arne Duncan delivered a speech to an audience of college students at Columbia University. The purpose of the speech was to both motivate and inspire America's future teachers. As he spoke, he explained the heightened responsibilities of the 21st-century educator: "In our new era of accountability, it is not enough for a teacher to say, 'I taught it—but the students didn't learn it.' As Linda Darling-Hammond has pointed out, that is akin to saying 'the operation was a success but the patient died.'"[34]

The comparison Mr. Duncan made between a teacher and a surgeon was an interesting one. Surgeons, in general, are treated as specialists. They are regarded as experts in their field and are provided with a complex system of supports. When performing an operation, a surgeon is given a team of people to help him both prepare the patient and assist him during the procedure. Nurses take blood pressure, monitor vital signs, and give transfusions; anesthesiologists administer anesthetics; and radiographers take x-rays. And that's only in the hospital. If you go back to the surgeon's private office, you will find receptionists making reminder calls to patients about appointments and interns managing and updating files. There are also security guards on hand to deal with violent or confrontational patients.

Teachers, on the other hand, are jacks-of-all-trades. They teach and discipline and police and parent. They write and grade lessons, but they also make phone calls and make photocopies and monitor hallways and write progress reports. They calculate report card grades, compose syllabi, chaperone dances, and break up fights. They basically do everything that needs to be done in order for their students to learn. Their instruction is highly scrutinized and held to rigorous standards, but they are not treated as instructional *specialists*. In general, teachers are not given the supports necessary to allow them to wholly focus on their teaching.

Imagine if the surgeon performing the operation in the Arne Duncan analogy were expected to take his own x-rays, administer his own anesthesia, and deal with blood transfusions. Imagine if he were required to make all the phone calls to all the patients to remind them not to eat 12 hours before the surgery. On top of that, imagine if the surgeon were responsible for keeping order on the hospital floor. How might this affect his performance?

Some might say comparing teachers to medical doctors is absurd. Surgeons are highly skilled and their opinions are well respected. Teachers, on the other hand, are educational *grunts*, and their insights about their own profession are often dismissed by educational leaders as uninformed and taken with a grain of salt. Teachers are of low social status and, therefore, not viewed as *experts*. They are not scholars or professors. They are not researchers or social scientists. They have not achieved any high status associated with politics or the writing of educational policy. If they had, they wouldn't still be in the K–12 classroom. So how seriously should they be taken?

The answer, as evidenced by their place in the educational pecking order, is not very seriously. Think about it. Education is one of the only professions in America where the policy is written and the decisions are made by a governing body *outside* of the field. Doctors, lawyers, and engineers all police themselves. Their panels and boards of directors are made up of other doctors, lawyers, and engineers. The same holds true for counselors and carpenters and plumbers and electricians and dentists. Even professors and researchers are subject to a peer review.

Not teachers. *Politicians* make decisions when it comes to education in K–12 schools. So do researchers, think tanks, and lobbyists. Does it matter that these people have little to no experience teaching in a K–12 classroom? No, it doesn't. Why? Because these folks have the power, and they have the *data*. They have *numbers*. And what do the teachers have to offer? Just experience. Just thousands of hours of trial and error, of dealing with children, parents, principals, curriculum, instructional strategies, educational pedagogy, and all manner of trainings and workshops. That's all the teachers bring to the table. Unfortunately, these contributions aren't data driven, lack political backing, and aren't subject to peer review. As a result, they aren't given much value.

Traditionally, implementing educational policy is something politicians do *to* teachers, not *with* them. Vicki L. Phillips, the director of education initiatives at the Bill and Melinda Gates Foundation, admits that this is an issue. "Teachers make up the bulk of the staffing in districts and schools, and they are the anchor of the profession. It seems to us their voices ought to really count," she says in a 2010 *Education Week* article.[35]

In the same article, Raegen T. Miller, a senior policy analyst for the Washington think tank Center on American Progress, says, "For a while, we've been ramping up accountability without really getting into what's going on in the school. We can do better than stand on the outside of the black box and look at a few numbers spit out by the annual tests, and see what rewards and sanctions make sense."[36]

What makes sense is treating teachers like specialists. What makes sense is listening to their voices and using all of their experiences and expertise to reform educational policy. What makes sense is valuing their opinions, especially when it comes to providing the kinds of educational supports needed to help our nation's children succeed.

NOTES

1. Thomas G. Carroll, "The High Cost of Teacher Turnover," National Commission on Teaching and America's Future, June 2007, www.nctaf.org/resources/demonstration_projects/turnover/documents/NCTAFCostofTeacherTurnoverpolicybrief.pdf.
2. Carroll, "The High Cost of Teacher Turnover," 1.
3. Carroll, "The High Cost of Teacher Turnover," 3–5.
4. Carroll, "The High Cost of Teacher Turnover," 1.
5. Carroll, "The High Cost of Teacher Turnover," 1.
6. Ruth Curran Neild, Elizabeth Useem, and Elizabeth Farley, *The Quest for Quality: Recruiting and Retaining Teachers in Philadelphia* (Philadelphia, PA: Research for Action, 2005), www.researchforaction.org/wp-content/uploads/publication-photos/149/Neild_R_Quest_for_Quality.pdf, 6.
7. Neild, Useem, and Farley, *The Quest for Quality*, 7–8.
8. Neild, Useem, and Farley, *The Quest for Quality*, 9.
9. Kristen A. Graham, "Superintendent Arlene Ackerman Named Top Urban School Leader in the U.S." *Philadelphia Inquirer*, October 22, 2010.
10. School District of Philadelphia, Office of Teacher Affairs, http://webgui.phila.k12.pa.us/offices/t/teacher-affairs.
11. Kristen A. Graham, "Crime Hit Record Level in Phila. Schools During 2007–08," *Philadelphia Inquirer*, May 19, 2009.
12. Graham, "Crime Hit Record Level."
13. Graham, "Crime Hit Record Level."
14. Graham, "Crime Hit Record Level."
15. Kern Alexander and M. David Alexander, *American Public School Law*, 4th ed. (Belmont, CA: Wadsworth, 1998), 435.
16. Graham, "Crime Hit Record Level."
17. Editorial, "Can't Learn in Bad Schools," *Philadelphia Inquirer*, June 21, 2009.

18. Editorial, "Can't Learn in Bad Schools."
19. Stephen Sawchuk, "Merit-Pay Model Pushed by Duncan Shows No Achievement Edge," *Education Week*, June 9, 2010, 1, 21.
20. Stephen Sawchuk, "Merit Pay Found to Have Little Effect on Achievement," *Education Week*, September 21, 2010, www.edweek.org/ew/articles/2010/09/21/05pay_ep.h30.html?qs=performance+pay.
21. Cynthia Henry, "Christie Proposes Changes in How Teachers Are Paid, Promoted," *Philadelphia Inquirer*, September 29, 2010.
22. Margery Mayer and Vicki L. Phillips, *Primary Sources: America's Teachers on America's Schools* (Scholastic, 2010), www.scholastic.com/primarysources/pdfs/Scholastic_Gates_0310.pdf, 39.
23. Mayer and Phillips, *Primary Sources*, 43.
24. Dom Giordano, "The Myths Used to Oppose Merit Pay for New Jersey Teachers," *Philadelphia Daily News*, September 8, 2010.
25. Elizabeth Word, *State of Tennessee's Student/Teacher Achievement Ratio Project* (Nashville: Tennessee State University, Center of Excellence for Research in Basic Skills, November 1990), 17.
26. Gillian Cohen, Christine Miller, Robert Stonehill, and Claire Geddes, *The Class Size Reduction Program: Boosting Student Achievement in Schools Across the Nation; A First Year Report* (Jessup, MD: U.S. Department of Education, September 2000), www2.ed.gov/offices/OESE/ClassSize/class.pdf, 1.
27. Cohen et al., *The Class Size Reduction Program*, 1.
28. Cohen et al., *The Class Size Reduction Program*, 4–7.
29. Cohen et al., *The Class Size Reduction Program*, 8.
30. Brian M. Stecher, Daniel F. McCaffrey, and Delia Bugliari, "The Relationship between Exposure to Class Size Reduction and Student Achievement in California," *Education Policy Analysis Archives* 11, no. 40 (November 10, 2003), http://epaa.asu.edu/epaa/v11n40/, 21.
31. Dom Giordano, "Education's 5 Big Lies," *Philadelphia Daily News*, November 17, 2009.
32. The Associated Press, "Class-Size Debate over Flexibility, Funding," *St. Augustine Record*, October 14, 2010, http://staugustine.com/news/local-news/2010-10-14/class-size-debate-over-flexibility-funding.
33. Linda Jacobson, "Research: Sizing Up Small Classes," *Education Week*, February 28, 2001, 26–28.
34. Arne Duncan, "Teacher Preparation: Reforming the Uncertain Profession" (remarks, Teachers College, Columbia University, New York, October 22, 2009), U.S. Department of Education, www.ed.gov/news/speeches/teacher-preparation-reforming-uncertain-profession.
35. Stephen Sawchuk, "Teacher Polls Look to Sway Policymakers," *Education Week*, March 31, 2010, 18–19.
36. Sawchuk, "Teacher Polls Look to Sway Policymakers," 14–15.

SEVEN

A Day in the Life

The one thing I remember experiencing my first year on the job was exhaustion. Teaching was *tough*. To do it right, it demanded an incredible amount of your time. To do it right it had to become a *lifestyle*, a part of your very existence.

My typical day in 1997 was loaded. I'd get up at 5:30 a.m., shower, dress, eat, and walk out the door by 6:45 a.m. Most of my neighbor's cars were still in their driveways at this hour. Many of the people on the road were blue-collar guys—construction workers who drove trucks and carried thermoses and big lunch boxes. To me, there was always a side to teaching that was blue collar.

I'd arrive at school by 7:15 and sign in at the main office. I'd grab my roll book for my homeroom, check my mailbox for messages and other paperwork, and head to my classroom. If I had parents to call that day, I'd do this in the teacher's room on the only phone, hoping to catch a kid's mother before she went to work (this was before cell phones). At least one of the numbers I'd call would be disconnected and no longer in service. At least one of the numbers would be from a parent who didn't have the same last name as his or her child. I learned early on that if the student's name was, say, Mary Smith, you couldn't just call the child's house and ask for Mr. or Mrs. Smith; the odds were Mr. Smith didn't live there anymore and that Mrs. Smith was back to using her maiden name or the name of her new husband. Even more tragic, some of the students didn't even live with either of their parents but with a grandparent or some other foster care giver. The routine for calling a kid's house was to ask for the parent or guardian of the child: "Hello, may I speak to the parent or guardian of Mary Smith please?"

When I did get a parent on the line, I'd identify myself as Mr. Paslay, your child's English teacher, and go into the reason for the call. *Your child's been cutting*; or *your child's been misbehaving and distracting other students*; or *your child didn't turn in his or her persuasive essay that was due last Friday*. Parents responded to my calls in a number of ways. Some were concerned and insisted that they would open up a can of whoop-ass on their child as soon as they got home. Others sounded put out, like their lives were complicated enough already without some teacher hounding them on the phone. Once in a while, I'd get a hold of a parent who had thrown in the towel completely, admitting to me that they simply didn't know *what* to do with their son or daughter, that if I had any ideas, they were willing to listen.

After the phone calls, I'd go through my mail. Any forms to complete, progress reports or documents from the counselor, I'd put in the top drawer of my desk to complete when I had more time. I did the same with memos and other paperwork reminding me about scheduled meetings. Then I'd set up my room for first period. This involved putting notes up on the board, getting any video, audio, or computer equipment organized, and making sure all materials and supplies were in order. Were there enough copies of the book or magazine I was using that day? Were there enough newspapers and graphic organizers?

Before computerized grading, I had to set up my attendance and grade book for the day, recording the date, getting out seating charts if needed. Then I waited, ready for the students to arrive. It was important to be ready for their arrival, to have all things in place. If I was a step behind, if I was putting up notes on the board at the last minute or running around to get extra copies, I played catch-up the whole period. It was like the gun sounding and being stuck at the starting line, watching the race take off without me; it knocked me that much off my game.

When the bell rang, I stepped out into the hallway to greet the students at the door as they entered my room. I also pitched in to keep my end of the hallway clear, to keep the traffic moving. There was always a lot of congestion in the halls first thing in the morning: kids coming in late, congregating with friends, lollygagging and taking the long way everywhere. I'd shoo some students off to class only to see them circle back around a moment later. The hall monitor at the time, a short, 60-something woman named Florence, would holler and shout and tell the kids to move on, to take off their hats, but it usually took a good 10 minutes for the halls to calm down.

"Shut up, Florence!" the students would say, mocking the way she talked. Then they'd crack up laughing and wander off. Some mornings, I'd get in the fray, demanding they comply with the rules, but most times, this only insured that I'd start the morning off on the wrong foot, completely frustrated over a student who either ignored my directions or copped an attitude.

At the late bell, I'd come back into my classroom and shut the door. At this point, at least one student would ask to go to the bathroom or to his or her locker or go get a drink of water really fast before class got started. I'd say "No, sorry, not right now." We had things to do, and they needed to get started on them. I had freshman first period, so this meant reminding them to sit down in their seats and *relax*. Sit down, and get started on the journal entry that was written on the green board in the front of the room.

They'd settle and take out their journals. They'd complete the entry, reflecting on the topic and writing out their thoughts in at least *one paragraph*. A paragraph was a minimum of five sentences, I'd tell them. Journals were collected once a week and counted as 10 percent of their report card grade. I circulated the room and reminded them of the importance of the journals. I also tried to stimulate their thinking by pushing them to answer the question from different angles. Some students responded positively to this stimulation; others didn't want to be bothered and put their heads down. I'd ask them nicely to pick their heads up, and if they didn't cooperate, I'd confront them and put their names on my "call list." Occasionally, an argument broke out. Once in a blue moon, this led to someone cursing at me, at which point I pink-slipped the student and sent him or her to the discipline office.

Journal entries varied. There were always a handful of kids who didn't have pens or bring their notebooks. In order to keep them on task, I'd lend them looseleaf paper and let them borrow pens in exchange for allowing me to hold their student IDs for collateral. The same group of students forgot their pens and notebooks on a regular basis. Lending them the materials just encouraged their bad habits. I started charging a quarter for pens and paper, at which time these kids called me cheap and rebelled from completing journals altogether. I called their parents with varying degrees of success.

After the journals were completed, we discussed their responses. Topics that were very interesting and stimulating—like abortion or legalizing marijuana—sometimes broke into heated arguments. Despite my rules and specific instructions, five or six people spoke at once.

"Excuse me!" I'd shout. "One person at a time." I'd fight tooth and nail to get the class settled and refocused. I'd call on another student to share his journal. Thirty seconds later, the person speaking would get bombarded by an opposing opinion, then two, then ten. The room would erupt like Jerry Springer, minus the fights. I'd run out of energy and have to move to the next activity, even if there wasn't significant closure.

The next activity piggybacked the journal topic, which was geared toward the objectives for the day. If we were doing a short story from the literature textbook, I'd transition into a "before" reading activity—the KWL was my staple the first year. I'd have the students preview the title and look at the pictures in order to make predictions about what the story might be about. Next, we'd preview vocabulary, briefly going through the meanings of the difficult words found in the text.

Late students would begin arriving at this time, some of them showing up 30 minutes after the bell, strictly because their parents failed to get them out of bed and out the door in time for school. Despite my classroom rules, the student would swagger into the room obnoxiously, in the middle of conversations with someone in the hall, laughing, sometimes cursing, cross the front of the room, and go to his or her desk. On the way, the late student might stop and screw with friends.

Once seated, the student would ask, "What are we doing?" I'd explain the procedure for coming in late and tell the student to check the board for pre-class, for any journal entry to complete.

"You got a pen I can borrow?" he or she would ask.

"No. You need to be more organized. Where's your notebook?"

"I forgot it."

"I'll give you a pen and paper for 25 cents. You can pay me tomorrow if you don't have it. I'll write your name down."

We'd begin reading the story. I might start with the audio version, or we'd read the first page together as a class. Once the students were into the set-up of the plot, I'd have them read independently, using a QNT to deconstruct the text as they read. A QNT was a strategy that stood for "quotes, notes and thoughts." Much like a KWL, students took out a paper and folded it into threes and labeled it accordingly. Under Q, they recorded any quotes that struck them as interesting or important; under N, they took any notes about any particular passage that they either enjoyed or had questions about; and under T, they recorded thoughts and reflections about certain passages. It was designed to get them engaged with the reading.

Unfortunately, it didn't work so well. Getting students engaged with reading was perhaps the most challenging thing about being an English teacher. In the beginning, especially dealing with freshman, if we didn't read the story out loud as a class or listen to it on audio, the students tuned out. Many didn't have the self control or focus to read long passages on their own. They lasted no more than a few minutes and then started talking. I constantly had to circulate the room and raise my voice to get them back on task. This was before I learned about "chunking" and other kinds of literacy strategies. I was a rookie teacher and didn't know the tricks of the trade. I had limited supporting materials, and many of the things I did, many of my activities and methods of instruction, were worked out through trial and error.

By the end of the period, which at the time was 57 minutes long, we usually would have gone through at least three activities: a pre-class warm-up to introduce the topic for the day, a reading piece that was not always guided with a directed reading strategy, and a writing piece that was not always centered on the proper objectives and didn't build in that day's vocabulary. Often, I struggled with classroom management, so my activities were based not on the best methods of instruction or learning objectives but on what would keep the students the quietest. And I rarely gave homework. At the time, homework was incredibly hard to keep up with.

After first period, my gas tank was already half empty. If there were a confrontation or spat with a student, my energy would be totally spent. But there was no time for self-pity because as the bell rang and one class left, another took its place.

Second period was the same as the first—30 energetic freshman. I'd go out into the hall to greet them as they entered the room. There would be arguments over taking off hats and clearing the corridor. There would be lateness, kids coming in five or ten minutes after the bell with cans of soda they illegally purchased from the vending machines in the lunchroom. There would be more students without pens or notebooks, students who just wanted to screw off or put their heads down on the desk and sleep. And there would be complaining. Complaining over the journal entry, complaining over the story or article we had to read, complaining over the stupid writing assignment we had to do.

When second period left, third period came in. Same drill. Thirty freshmen acting like freshman. Arguing, complaining, challenging my authority. On bad days, I'd be running on fumes. I was physically *drained*, and sometimes it was quite a struggle just to get everyone's attention to begin the lesson. The kids would be in their seats with their journals out but still brimming with energy, poking each other, play fighting, horsing around like they were out on the playground. I'd stand at the front of the room, waiting for just the right moment to get started. The feeling was a mixture of anxiety and apprehension, like looking at a 200-pound television that you know you have to carry up five flights of steps. When I thought the time was right, I'd jump in and get started.

"Okay," I'd begin, "it's time to get started. I need everyone's attention now, guys. Seriously. Does anyone want to share their journal entry today?"

Nine out of ten times, the room didn't settle. Just *asking* for their attention usually didn't cut it. The freshmen were in their own little worlds, and conversation continued.

"Okay, guys," I'd say and start naming the names of the individuals who were still not listening. "Joe, I need your attention. Denise, Shakira, please. Let's stop the talking now . . ."

Sometimes Joe, or Denise, or Shakira would get mad and say, "What?! What do you *want*?!"

"Stop talking please."

"Man, I'm not the only one."

My patience would slip. So would my temper. I knew it was time to stop being nice; it was time to start lifting the 200-pound television up the five flights of steps. There are theories in textbooks that state teachers don't have to expend this kind of energy to get students' attention, that if they have established routines in the beginning of the year—such as flicking the lights on or off or holding up their index finger to signal silence—then students will comply practically effort free. But from my experience that first year, this was a lot of bologna. I'd flicked the lights on and off several times in September, only to have the freshman go, "Ooo! Haunted house!"

Frustration mounting, I'd raise my voice. "Excuse me!" I'd shout finally. "I need everyone quiet and facing forward, now!" Things would begin to settle; although, there were always a few pockets of students who refused to allow my lesson to interrupt their personal conversations. Then I would begin teaching.

Advisory, otherwise known as homeroom, would begin right after third period ended. Thirty more freshmen would flood my classroom, talking, goofing off, sometimes wrestling. My goal during advisory wasn't to keep them quiet but just to keep them in their seats. I'd sit at my desk and take attendance. In the beginning of the year, I'd ask students who were absent the day before if they had a note, but after a week of doing so, it became clear that bringing in a signed slip of paper from mom or dad was clearly the exception rather than the rule; to my shock, less than 10 percent of the students in my advisory ever had a note excusing their absence.

What's with these kids' parents? I would think to myself, remembering how concerned my own mother and father were with my education. Clearly, many of these children lacked the proper guidance. School was not a top priority at home, and the absence of their parents' involvement was having a negative effect on their overall study habits and learning.

Halfway through the 20-minute advisory period, the PA announcements would come on.

"Shhhh!" I'd tell them. "Let's listen. This is important."

Not many people listened or cared.

After advisory was my 45-minute lunch period. I'd eat my sandwich, take the roll book back down to the main office, and get ready for the last two classes of the day. I'd straighten my room (pick up the crumpled paper, candy wrappers, and the occasional empty soda can) and replenish supplies. With time left over, I'd grade papers or think about preparing activities for the next day.

The bell would ring. Another 30 freshman—my fourth class of the day—would come through the door. Like me, most had just finished their lunch. Most days, this group had two gears: (1) bouncing off the walls and (2) sleeping. There was no in-between. Because of the sugar rush from lunch, they had even more energy than the group before them. Getting their attention at the beginning of class was the equivalent of carrying a *300*-pound television up to the attic, if you can believe that. Fortunately, I'd have a second wind from eating as well, so I'd usually be able to pull off the task of getting them quiet and writing in their journals.

But often, forcing them to shut down and concentrate had an interesting effect on their bodies: it sent them into second gear—sleep mode.

If they couldn't bounce around and talk and burn off the sugar with no holds barred, many times they shut down. Bang. Out like a light. Snoring and drooling on the desk. I was absolutely stunned and amazed at how little ability they had to control themselves, to put up with just a minimal amount of discomfort. I was also amazed at how many parents of these children seemed to suffer from the same issues.

On days that I was struggling to get through the period, I'd cave in and let 25 percent of the class sleep. I welcomed the peace and quiet. I was presenting the lesson to whoever wanted to get an education. If they opted out, so be it. It was their choice.

Next period was my 57-minute prep. If I could muster the energy, I'd get started on making copies for the next day. I might call a parent if there was an incident earlier in the day or continue grading papers. Many times, I just vegged out at my desk and tried to keep my sanity. I was fried and often did a lot of staring out into space.

The last period of the day was sophomores. This group of 29 students was a little more mature than my first four classes of ninth graders. They actually entered my room like regular human beings. This had a lot to do with the fact that 15 to 20 percent of them cut the class every day; it was the last period, and many wanted to go home early. At first, I spent an incredible amount of time chasing down cuts—checking attendance in advisory roll books and speaking with other teachers (back then, there was no computerized attendance system)—but after a few months, I didn't have the time or energy to waste on kids who didn't want to be in school.

Because the school didn't have any 10th-grade literature textbooks, I photocopied a lot of material out of my college intro-to-literature anthology to use with the sophomores. I also adapted the writing assignments I used with the ninth graders to use with the tenth graders. By this point in the day, I was burnt. Cashed. Out of steam. So were the students. Because of my lack of experience and the lack of materials, my lessons were often thin and didn't last the full 57-minute period. Often, by 2:30, 15 minutes before the bell, there'd be nothing to do. Students would talk and congregate in clusters in the room. I'd yell and tell them to get back in their seats, but this was a struggle. They were bored and ready to go home. Five full minutes before the bell, they'd line up at the door, waiting. Sometimes they'd push through the doorway and spill out into the hallway.

"Wait for the bell," I'd tell them and have to stand in the doorway to keep them from sneaking off. Every so often, I'd get tired of the routine and make a new rule: no one could leave at the bell unless everybody was seated. It worked for about a week, but I soon ran out of energy and lost the ability to enforce the rule. At the bell, people left anyway. I gave detentions and made calls but again got limited results.

When the bell finally rang to end the day, the feeling of relief was incredible. The television was safely on the fifth floor of the apartment (some days, I'll admit, I only got it to the third floor), and now I could put it down and catch my breath.

Of course, the end of class didn't mean the end of my day. There was still an incredible amount of work to be completed before it was quitting time. Papers to grade. Lessons to write. Calls to make to parents to try to get them involved in their child's education in any way I could. Some days, there were after-school meetings with special education teachers to fill out individualized education plans (IEPs) or conferences with administrators to work on comprehensive support assistant programs (CSAPs). After it was all said and done, I'd leave school sometimes as late as 5:00 p.m.

When you do the math, I was working close to a 10-hour day.

EIGHT
Family and the Community

In 1994, Anne T. Henderson and Nancy Berla published a book called *A New Generation of Evidence: The Family Is Critical to Student Achievement*. In it, they analyze 66 noteworthy studies, reviews, reports, and books on the correlation between family involvement and student success in school. "When parents are involved in their children's education at home, their children do better in school," they conclude. "When parents are involved at school, their children go farther in school, and the schools they go to become better."[1] The authors also find that a home environment that encourages learning is more important to student achievement than income, education level, or cultural background.[2]

In addition, Henderson and Berla note that several themes emerged throughout the studies they analyzed: school reform is much more effective if it includes families; children whose parents are involved in school stay longer in school; children do best when their parents act as supporters, advocates, and decision makers; the better the partnership between families and schools, the higher the student achievement; and the best results are achieved when families, community organizations, and schools all work together.[3]

Parental involvement is particularly important in early childhood. In their groundbreaking book, *Meaningful Differences in the Everyday Experience of Young American Children*, Betty Hart and Todd R. Risley show that the achievement gap between the suburban middle class and the urban underprivileged starts even before kindergarten. Their research indicates that a child's cognitive development is greatly influenced by the type of interaction he or she has with his or her parents. The amount and kind of language children hear in infancy is strongly correlated with their IQs later in life. They also found that discipline at home has a major impact on a child's intelligence. Facing a lot of prohibition and discouragement has a negative effect on IQ, whereas affirmation and encouragement have a positive effect on learning.[4]

The impact of the home environment on student achievement is well documented. The family is an educational ally America must strive harder to embrace.

THE WELL-BEING OF CHILDREN IN AMERICA

Research continues to show that the well-being of children—their health and safety, material security, and sense of being loved and valued by their family—has a significant effect on their ability to learn. Yet in the United States, the well-being of children is surprisingly low compared to other parts of the world.

In 2007, UNICEF issued a report on the lives and well-being of children in economically advanced nations called *Child Poverty in Perspective: An Overview of Child Well-Being in Rich Countries*. The study looks at children and young people living in 21 of the world's industrialized nations and provides a comprehensive assessment of their well-being in six different categories.

In the category of *material well-being*, the United States ranked 17th out of 21. In particular, child poverty in America was over 15 percent. Children affected by poverty in the United States had high levels of deprivation, which meant they and their families lacked many of the basic things needed to be successful in school, such as a computer, a desk, a quiet place to study, a dictionary, a calculator, and school texts.[5] The report notes:

> The evidence from many countries persistently shows that children who grow up in poverty are more vulnerable: specifically, they are more likely to be in poor health, to have learning and behavioral difficulties, to underachieve at school, to become pregnant at too early an age, to have lower skills and aspirations, to be low paid, unemployed, and welfare dependent.[6]

America was dead last in the second dimension of the study, *health and safety*. In particular, the United States had a comparatively high infant mortality rate and low infant birth weight; the United States ranked in the middle on immunizations. When it came to deaths from accidents and injuries, the United States ranked second to last behind New Zealand.[7]

The third dimension of the UNICEF report, *educational well-being*, found that the United States ranked 12th out of 21. American children placed in the bottom third in achievement in reading, math, and science. Data also reveal that less than 80 percent of U.S. 15- to 19-year-olds were engaged in full-time or part-time education. More startling was the fact that over 30 percent of 15-year-olds in the United States expected to find future employment that required only "low skills."[8]

The United States ranked second to last in dimension four, *relationships*. America had the highest percentage of young people living in single-parent families. The report notes "at the statistical level there is evidence to associate growing up in single-parent families and stepfamilies with greater risk to well-being—including a greater risk of dropping out of school, of leaving home early, of poorer health, of low skills, and of low pay." In addition, only about 65 percent of 15-year-olds from the United States reported eating the main meal of the day "several times per week" with their parents. And only 55 percent of American children found their peers to be "kind and helpful."[9]

The United States also ranked second to last when it came to dimension five, *behavior and risks*. Less than half of American young people reported eating breakfast every school day, less than 30 percent reported eating fruit daily, over 25 percent reported being overweight, over 30 percent admitted using marijuana in the past year, and 35 percent reported being involved in fighting in the past year.[10]

According to UNICEF, "The true measure of a nation's standing is how well it attends to its children—their health and safety, their material security, their education and socialization, and their sense of being loved, valued, and included in the families and societies into which they are born."[11]

When it comes to the well-being of children, the Unites States is far from a world leader.

EMBRACING THE EVIDENCE

For decades, researchers and social scientists have compiled numerous reports highlighting the importance of family and community involvement in education. The Educational Testing Service's 1992 policy report titled *America's Smallest School: The Family*, authored by Paul E. Barton and Richard J. Coley, reveals some interesting information regarding the home as an educational institution. In the report, the authors show how factors such as reading at home, watching television, completing homework, getting children to school, and the amount of books in a home all significantly impact on a student's education and academic achievement.[12]

In light of these findings, the report makes it very clear that education reform in America mustn't be limited to schools but must also include the home. The authors offer four recommendations: national goals in education will be difficult to achieve without educational reform in the home; state-by-state rankings should not only focus on schools but also on home environment; to make big gains in academic achievement, America's attitude toward education must change, and this change must start in the home; and government policies on welfare dependency and child poverty should also be viewed as *education* policies because they have such a significant impact on home and school.[13]

In 2007, Barton and Coley did a follow-up report to their 1992 study. In addition to providing new evidence from a multitude of new sources on the importance of family in regard to education, the authors make an unfortunate observation: not much has been done in the past 25 years to include the family in education reform.[14] In other words, policies on education—especially at the state and federal levels—had, for the most part, ignored the home environment. There was no national resolve, the authors say, to improve the family as an educational institution.

Barton and Coley state, "Although the critical importance children's families play in their lives in the years preceding school, during the hours before and after the school day, and throughout the days, weeks, and months of summer and holiday breaks remains apparent, it also stays largely outside current local, state, and national education policy discussions."[15]

It seems apparent that government leaders find statistics about home environment messy and uncomfortable. Politicians—those who introduce much of America's educational policy—rarely include families as part of school reform. Part of this may have to do with the fact that school reform should focus on *schools*; everyone knows there is much room for improvement there. But another reason for ignoring the importance of families might have to do with politics. Holding parents and communities accountable for contributing to the education of America's children is not only politically incorrect but also could very well turn off voters and members of certain constituency groups. It's much cleaner to embrace society's anti-teacher, anti-school mentality and keep a narrow focus on reforming education the traditional way.

Think about it. How often do those running for office announce that, in America, only 68 percent of children live with two parents? How often do they break the news that in the black community, only 35 percent of children live with two parents? How often do they admit that children in single-mother families score lower on academic tests, have higher incidences of psychological problems that reflect aggression and poor conduct, have a greater tendency to abuse illegal substances, are more likely to have sexual relationships at an earlier age, and have lower self-esteem than children from two-parent families?[16]

How often do they chastise parents for their failure to read to their children? How often do they acknowledge that there are major differences in the vocabularies of the rich and the poor? How often do they acknowledge that by age four, to quote Barton and Coley, "the average child in a professional family hears about 20 million more words than the average child in a working-class family, and about 35 million more words than children in welfare families"?[17]

How often do you hear politicians tout that 19 percent of children live in poverty in America, and one out of every three black children is impoverished? That 11 percent of U.S. homes are "food insecure" and that this rate is triple for black children? That 44 percent of American women aged 30 or under have out-of-wedlock births?[18] Or that 1.5 million parents have at one time in their lives been incarcerated in a state or federal prison?[19] The answer is that you *don't* hear it.

This *denial*, if you will, is no doubt hampering efforts at education reform. It also might explain why a significant portion of Barton and Coley's work—much of which brings attention to the importance of family and societal factors in education—is given only token attention by politicians, the media, and the public at large.

The coverage of *Parsing the Achievement Gap II*, a 2009 report by Barton and Coley that studied the causes of the racial achievement gap in America, is a perfect example of the media's selective reporting. In May of 2009, shortly after the study was released, *Education Week* did an article on the report. Interestingly, of the 16 factors Barton and Coley list in their paper as problems contributing to the skills gap between black and white students, *Education Week* only writes about 6.[20] Four of the six are criticisms of schools and teachers, while the other two briefly mention the issues of television watching and exposure to lead. Of the 10 factors passed over by *Education Week,* eight relate to home environment.[21]

The *Philadelphia Public School Notebook*, an independent newspaper dedicated to covering Philadelphia public schools, did much of the same with the winter 2006 issue titled "Focus on Parental Involvement." Although their stories and editorials cover everything from the varying types of parental involvement to parent activism around the city, their issue for the most part ignores the 25 years of research complied by Barton and Coley.[22] Their articles fail to adequately address the need for parents to read to their children, for parents to regulate the television, for parents to establish a quiet place in the home for children to complete homework, and for parents to provide their children with proper nutrition.

The *Notebook*'s focus on parental involvement is, for the most part, *school centered* and, by and large, criticizes schools for not being "welcoming" or "accommodating" enough for parents. Like most media covering home environment, they fail to make an effort to improve *family* as an educational institution.

For school reform to truly work, writers of education policy must better incorporate the home and family.

COMMUNITIES AND SCHOOLS: THE CHICKEN AND EGG DEBATE

What came first, the community or the school? Or, put another way, do communities stem from schools or do schools stem from communities? The answer to this question, unlike the quandary concerning the origin of poultry, is not hard to answer.

Schools clearly are the product of communities. History proves this fact. In the late 1400s, when the first Europeans landed in North America, there did not already exist American schools on the continent. Granted, there were Native Americans who educated their young, but *American schools* didn't exist. Neither Christopher Columbus nor Amerigo Vespucci got off their ships and found erected in the forest red-brick buildings with steeples and bells and big wooden doors. They didn't come ashore and say, "Hey! What are those things over there? Are they schools? You know, I think they are! Cool! Now we can send our kids to them!"

History tells us this didn't happen. Schools didn't magically appear out of thin air—they did not spontaneously create themselves in a vacuum cut off from the rest of civilization. No, schools were created by communities and societies looking to educate their *own*. They were conceived, designed, built, funded, and staffed *for* the people, *by* the people.

Although Puritan settlers educated their own children by teaching them to read and write in their own homes, America's first public school, Boston Latin School, was founded in 1635 by the town of Boston.[23] The town assigned public funds to support the school. In 1642, Massachusetts Bay Colony passed the first education law, which states that all children must learn to read and write.[24] In 1647, they passed another law: all towns must establish and maintain public schools. This was done so men could read and interpret the Bible and understand the laws governing society.[25]

American independence marked a change in education. After the Revolutionary War, Thomas Jefferson had a new vision for public schools. His plan for Virginia in 1782 involved dividing up the state into parcels about five square miles big and building a school in each where children from that area could attend.[26] Tuition would be covered by the state for those unable to pay.

In the first half of the 1800s, Horace Mann, viewed by some as one of the most important reformers of public education, worked tirelessly to upgrade conditions of public schools, increase school hours, improve the quality of teachers, and provide the public with better access to schools, among other things. Citizens took Mann's lead and worked hard to keep schools running effectively. In a companion piece to the documentary series *The Story of American Public Education*, PBS describes on their website how classrooms were maintained by the townspeople in the 1800s:

> The power of community and the high value placed on education are evident in the shared efforts involved in maintaining the schools. Farmers supplied the wood or other fuel for the stove to keep the schoolroom warm in the winter. Parents built school desks and took turns cleaning and stocking the stable that housed the horses the children used to get to and from school each day. Teachers often lived with local families, rotating from household to household.[27]

As education progressed into the 20th century, it became clear communities and their access to resources was impacting on the quality of their public schools. This was evident during the pre-1950s in the South. Segregation denied black communities basic needs, and their schools suffered horribly. White communities, on the other hand, were granted access to all the fruits of the American dream, and their schools performed accordingly.

In the 21st century, more than 50 years after the Civil Rights Act began breaking the bonds of racial discrimination and the Elementary and Secondary Education Act began funneling billions of dollars into high-poverty schools, kids are still not receiving equal educations. Often, these low performing schools reside in communities with high concentrations of poverty.

It's in these communities that citizens argue the opposite side of the community-school debate: the stability and quality of life in communities stem from the quality of the schools. As Geoffrey Canada often states, *education* is the only way out. *Schools* are the beacon light of hope for the disenfranchised and underprivileged. Although few will disagree with Canada about the power of education, there is one small problem: schools don't exist in a vacuum. They are interconnected and powered in a very real way by the communities they serve. Neighborhood school boards decide policies, hire and fire staff, and make important budgetary decisions. Parents partner with teachers and assist in the learning process. Local businesses provide internships and help place students in jobs. Churches hold fund raisers, and community groups advocate for high standards. Without these fundamental supports, schools suffer.

"Long before schools begin their jobs, however, teaching and learning take place in the family," Barton and Coley state in their 2007 report. "The quality of that home and family teaching makes a large difference in how much children know and how ready they are to learn when they get to school."[28]

The cycle of poverty is tragic because it is a catch-22: you need a good school to save a community, but you need a good community to save a school. Unless you find a way to transplant outside variables, such as Geoffrey Canada is doing for a small group of neighborhoods in Harlem, the process of change in high-poverty neighborhoods is going to be very slow. And by that time, thousands of students may already be lost.

Chapter 8

MEETING HALFWAY

Unlike many children in America today, I was blessed to grow up in a middle-class, two-parent family. My mother and father stressed education and made learning a priority. I vividly remember my parents attending report card conferences every single year and having at least a basic relationship with every one of my teachers. There was a routine for homework, and either my mother or father regularly checked my essays and tests when they were returned to me by my teachers.

My parents also got involved in school in other ways: they chaperoned trips and attended sporting events; whenever I was absent, they personally called my school's main office and sent me in the next day with a signed excusal note; they signed and promptly returned tests, quizzes, progress reports, report cards; they signed and promptly returned insurance forms, medical clearances for sports teams, and permission slips for field trips; they promptly returned phone calls from the school and collaborated with teachers to facilitate my academic improvement; and they sent me to school every day well rested, well fed, and with the proper supplies.

When I began teaching in Philadelphia, I quickly learned that not all children were as fortunate as I was. In large urban cities, where families are dealing with unemployment, domestic violence, addiction issues, and all manner of social ills, education is not always a priority. This reality hit home for me in the fall of 1997 when Swenson held its annual report card night for parents. The date was announced in the student handbook in the beginning of the year, and reminder letters were sent home with students in homerooms a week in advance. On the night of the conference, I received a grand total of six parents. At the time, I was teaching close to 150 students. *Where is everyone?* I wondered, shocked by the dismal turnout. Later that night, after the conference ended, I was informed by colleagues that this was par for the course; on a good night, a teacher could expect to meet about 10 percent of his students' parents.

The same kind of percentages existed when it came to chaperoning trips and attending school events—about 10 percent of the parents were involved. Paperwork was the same way: no more than 10 percent of students had absent notes, returned insurance forms, completed medical clearances for sports teams, and so forth. In the beginning of October, when I mailed failure notices out to 35 students with the instructions *Sign and return to your child's teacher within three days*, I received five forms back.

Student cuts were the most troubling. Although there was a core group of mothers and fathers who kept the lines of communication open with the school, too many parents didn't have a handle on their children's attendance. In 2009, according to statistics compiled by the *Phila-*

delphia Inquirer, 7,500 Philadelphia public school students on average played hooky every day.[29] Obviously, teachers can't help students if they don't even make it through the front door in the morning. Although some suggest truancy is the fault of boring teachers and a disorganized school culture, parents no doubt play a part.

There are a number of reasons why parents struggle when it comes to education. Over the last decade, I've spoken with dozens of mothers and fathers who have legitimate issues when it comes to actively participating in their children's schools. Some parents, because of English language issues, can't read letters sent by schools inviting them to attend conferences; some parents do not receive information far enough in advance to adjust their work schedules; cultural barriers make it difficult for some parents to be involved; some schools are not clear in terms of how much and in what ways they want parents involved; and some mothers and fathers have complained that schools are not "welcoming" enough to parents, that principals and teachers intimidate them or make them feel uncomfortable.

The Philadelphia School District has been working hard to solve these problems. In recent years, they've actively campaigned for better parental involvement. In 2008, Superintendent Ackerman developed the district's five "core beliefs," the second of which is the declaration that "Parents are our partners." Dr. Ackerman also helped develop Parent University, a free, educational program that offers skill-building classes for mothers and fathers who had children in the city's public schools. As of 2010, Parent University served more than 12,000 parents at 23 different class sites, and the program was recognized nationally in *Time* magazine. Dr. Ackerman also hired 170 parent ombudsmen to facilitate and encourage parent involvement throughout the city and opened a translation and interpretation center that translates district materials into eight different languages.[30]

With this said, however, there still needs to be a "balance" of responsibility between parents and schools. In other words, schools can't replace families. Those familiar with urban education in the 21st century understand that such an aim has been steadily gaining momentum. Education reformers are fighting to increase the length of the school day from 8 hours to 10 and have proposed holding school on Saturdays and during the summer months; this is clearly an attempt to make up for a lack of adequate parenting.

Reformers are also fighting to hold public schools responsible for a child's nutrition. In October of 2009, to help more children take advantage of the Philadelphia School District's free breakfast program, Dr. Ackerman implemented a new policy that made breakfast participation a part of a principal's performance rating. Incredibly *principals*—not parents—were being held accountable for students showing up to school in the morning and eating the free breakfast.[31]

The tragedy, of course, is that if a child's parents aren't held accountable for performing the most minimum of tasks—such as getting their child to school on time to receive a free meal—what is happening when it comes to helping with homework? What is happening when it comes to attending school functions? Teaching work ethic? Discipline? Respect?

Both schools and families are an integral part of a child's schooling. As such, neither one should be written out of the education equation.

PERSONAL VERSUS POLITICAL INVOLVEMENT

In the winter 2008 issue, the *Philadelphia Public School Notebook* wrote an editorial titled, "Building Parent Power." In it, the *Notebook* calls for parent leaders across the city "to come together and lay the foundation for a stronger network of organizations giving voice to their concerns." The *Notebook* praises organizations like ACORN and Eastern Pennsylvania Organizing Project for their advocacy work in education and for "developing new leaders and activists, helping parents deepen their understanding of issues, and challenging District leaders to make improvements."[32]

In my experience as an educator, there are two kinds of parental involvement: *personal* and *political*. Personal involvement is where parents become actively engaged in being good parents: teaching their children how to communicate and solve problems nonviolently, focusing on nutrition and setting a reasonable curfew, instilling in their sons and daughters work ethic and an appreciation for the value of education, and so forth. Political involvement is where parents become activists and organize for political reform: they challenge district leaders to change policies and network to make their voices and concerns heard. Many community groups place their focus on the latter and ignore the former. They call for parents to become politically active in the school system but fail to demand that moms and dads get personally involved in the educations of their sons and daughters at a home level.

Parents are an important part of education, not simply because they can protest for educational reform but because they can use their influence with their own children to make America's youth better students and citizens. If we truly want to build "parent power," we must start by doing so in the *home*. Every one of us must crawl before we can walk. According to Abraham Maslow's hierarchy of needs, we must satisfy physiological and safety needs—as well as the need for love and belonging—before we can satisfy the need for esteem. In other words, moms and dads must parent first, then they can get up on their political soapbox and advocate for reform.

Philadelphia's recent Parent Leadership Academy (PLA) is a case in point. A pilot effort by the Philadelphia School District and the William

Penn Foundation, PLA was formed to empower parents and promote them as leaders in their children's education and schools. Although PLA made some progress and was a valuable learning experience, in the end, the program was dropped because it didn't develop according to expectations.

In a 2008 report published by Research for Action titled *Parent Leadership Academy: A Parent-Led, District-Hosted Partnership for Parent Engagement*, researchers conclude, that ultimately, PLA "was not a sufficient lever for changing the District's relationship with parents."[33] One reason PLA failed was because parents couldn't move beyond the historic distrust of district officials and continued to complain that the climate was not "parent friendly." There was also tension between PLA board members and those involved in the Philadelphia Home and School Council.

There have been questions raised as to why a similar program in Kentucky—called the Center for Parental Leadership (one of the programs on which PLA was based)—is a reigning success and why PLA ultimately ended in failure. The answer may rest with Maslow's hierarchy of needs: parents in Kentucky, unlike many in Philadelphia, had established workable relationships at a base level—with their own families and communities—and thus possessed the tools and credibility necessary to take that next step toward educational activism.

So what are the solutions? How do we get parents of Philadelphia public school children involved at the home level so they can ultimately achieve that next step and get active in the district? According to the findings by Research for Action, providing educational programs for parents can help them get more involved with their child's schooling. "Increases in educational attainment for younger and less educated mothers are related to gains in children's achievement, particularly reading skills," the report explains.[34] It also finds that the more educated parents are, the more they are able to provide help with homework and become academic role models for their children; the Philadelphia School District's Parent University is ultimately helping with this.

In addition, neighborhood school-based sites are more effective in drawing parents than non-neighborhood school-based sites. Basically, participation by parents is highest at a site with a strong connection to the surrounding community. Moving beyond school walls is also a promising strategy for reaching parents. Instead of schools inviting parents to come to them, there should be a more community-based focus, and the district should reach parents where they are.

Parental involvement is a two-tier process. Parents must get involved at the home level in order to build the base necessary to get active in the district.

NOTES

1. Anne T. Henderson and Nancy Berla, *A New Generation of Evidence: The Family Is Critical to Student Achievement* (Washington DC: Center for Law and Education, 1997), 1.
2. Henderson and Berla, *A New Generation of Evidence*, 2–13.
3. Henderson and Berla, *A New Generation of Evidence*, 14–16.
4. Betty Hart and Todd R. Risley, *Meaningful Differences in the Everyday Experience of Young American Children* (Baltimore, MD: P. H. Brookes, 1995), 109–111.
5. UNICEF, "Child Poverty in Perspective: An Overview of Child Well-Being in Rich Countries," *Innocenti Report Card 7* (UNICEF Innocenti Research Centre, Florence, Italy, 2007), 5, www.unicef-irc.org/publications/445.
6. UNICEF, "Child Poverty in Perspective," 5.
7. UNICEF, "Child Poverty in Perspective," 12.
8. UNICEF, "Child Poverty in Perspective," 18.
9. UNICEF, "Child Poverty in Perspective," 22.
10. UNICEF, "Child Poverty in Perspective," 26.
11. UNICEF, "Child Poverty in Perspective," 1.
12. Paul E. Barton and Richard J. Coley, *America's Smallest School: The Family*, (Princeton, NJ: Educational Testing Service, 1992), www.ets.org/Media/Research/pdf/PICSMSCHOOL.pdf.
13. Barton and Coley, *America's Smallest School*, 3.
14. Paul E. Barton and Richard J. Coley, *The Family: America's Smallest School*, (Princeton, NJ: Educational Testing Service, September, 2007), www.ets.org/Media/Research/pdf/PICFAMILY.pdf.
15. Barton and Coley, *The Family*, 6.
16. Barton and Coley, *The Family*, 9.
17. Barton and Coley, *The Family*, 3.
18. Barton and Coley, *The Family*, 3.
19. Paul E. Barton and Richard J. Coley, *The Black-White Achievement Gap: When Progress Stopped* (Princeton, NJ: Educational Testing Service, July, 2010), 26, http://ets.org/Media/Research/pdf/PICBWGAP.pdf.
20. Debra Viadero, "ETS Tracks Causes of Scoring Gaps," *Education Week*, May 13, 2009, 5.
21. Paul E. Barton and Richard J. Coley, *Parsing the Achievement Gap II* (Princeton, NJ: Educational Testing Service, April, 2009), 3–4, www.ets.org/Media/Research/pdf/PICPARSINGII.pdf.
22. "Focus on Parental Involvement," *Philadelphia Public School Notebook* 14, no. 2 (Winter 2006).
23. Boston Latin School, "History: 375 Years," www.bls.org/podium/default.aspx?t=113646 (accessed October 2, 2010).
24. Kern Alexander and M. David Alexander, *American Public School Law*, 4th ed. (Belmont, CA: Wadsworth, 1998), 22.
25. Alexander and Alexander, *American Public School Law*, 4:22.
26. Gerald W. Bracey, *Education Hell: Rhetoric vs Reality* (Alexandria, VA: Educational Research Service, 2009), 17.
27. PBS, "Evolving Classroom," www.pbs.org/kcet/publicschool/evolving_classroom/index.html .
28. Barton and Coley, *The Family*, 39.
29. Editorial, "A Cost to Skip School," *Philadelphia Inquirer*, April 13, 2009.
30. School District of Philadelphia, *Imagine 2014: A Year 2 Update* (Philadelphia, PA: School Reform Commission, School District of Philadelphia, July 2010), 7, http://webgui.phila.k12.pa.us/uploads/Ii/j2/Iij2xbPsxRBWziF6LH6NLw/Priorities-Progress-Promises_Compressed.pdf.
31. Christopher Paslay, "Breakfast Shouldn't Be on the Principals," *Philadelphia Inquirer*, October 13, 2009.

32. Editorial, "Building Parent Power," *Philadelphia Public School Notebook* 16, no. 2 (Winter 2008).

33. Tracey A. Hartmann and Cecily A. Mitchell, *Parent Leadership Academy: A Parent-Led, District-Hosted Partnership for Parent Engagement* (Philadelphia, PA: Research for Action, September 2008), 1, http://researchforaction.org/.

34. Hartmann and Mitchell, *Parent Leadership Academy*, 5.

NINE

Revelation

When I returned to Swenson after the summer of 1998, I was a wreck. I knew deep down that if this school year turned out to be a repeat of the last, I wouldn't make it to Christmas. I refused to allow myself to deal with all the nonsense. The job simply wasn't worth it. If need be, I'd put in a request to be transferred from Swenson or just quit altogether.

There did, however, burn a small fire in the pit of my stomach. I *wasn't* a quitter, and by nature, I was very competitive. Although I felt no real thrill teaching English anymore, I knew what the world was like outside—especially the job market—and I knew I had to resist my impulse to pack up and leave Swenson; I'd give it one more honest shot.

I forced myself to keep an open mind. I had a year's experience under my belt, and this was *something*. I also had a year's worth of lesson plans and materials, and I was slowly, through trial and error, beginning to figure out what worked and what didn't. Deep down in my mind, I even had insights into *why* things turned out in class the way they did; of course, it would take months of reflection to fully extract and expound upon this knowledge.

After I greeted the staff and made small talk that morning, I picked up my roster in the main office. The first thing that jumped out at me was my class sizes: not a single one of my classes had more than 21 students; my sixth period only had 17. Was there some mistake? I hoped not. If these numbers were correct, there was a chance for me after all.

When classes started and I met my students, things ran smoothly the first week as they had the year before. It was the phenomenon of having freshman—the *honeymoon period*. I set up my rules and seating charts and tried to keep a positive attitude. I jumped right into a writing assignment, the five-paragraph persuasive essay. We talked about current events and had debates. After a week, I had a feeling that things *were* going to be different from last year. I was not only older and wiser, but the *students* seemed different as well. They seemed like a nicer group, more pleasant and respectful.

On top of this, I was beginning to understand a very important truth about teaching: I might not always be able to control my students, but I could control the way I *responded* to them. That was the key. When tempers flared, I didn't need to butt heads and try to compete. I could stay above the fray—take a step back and become a neutral observer. This way, I could disarm my students, get past the walls they so often constructed, and learn how to put my finger on their soft spots.

During the second week of school, I had a chance to put this new wisdom to the test. I was preparing to read Liam O'Flaherty's short story "The Sniper" with the class, so as a pre-reading exercise, the students needed to take the nine vocabulary words from the story and write them in original sentences using the definitions from the text.

A girl named Latoya was having trouble putting the word *remorse* in a sentence. I explained to her that she was using it incorrectly, and she copped an attitude.

"Man, this stuff is *stupid*," she said. She threw her paper on the floor. I opened my mouth to holler at her but closed it again. I took a mental deep breath. Then I did something that I normally wouldn't do: I had a sense of humor.

I calmly picked her paper up off the floor and put it back on her desk.

"I'm not doin' this stuff," she insisted. "I hate these vocabulary words."

"Why do you hate these vocab words?" I asked her. "What did these vocab words ever do to you?"

Latoya just looked at me.

"Did these vocabulary words talk trash about your boyfriend?"

Latoya cracked a smile. "Mr. Paslay, you *crazy*."

"I know I am," I told her. "But I still want to try to teach you this stuff. Vocabulary words are real important. Here, let's look at the word *remorse*. What part of speech is it?"

She checked her book. "It's a noun."

"Exactly, it's a noun. And what's a noun?"

"A person, place, or thing."

"Yes, and in this case, *remorse* is a *thing*. It's something you *feel*."

"It's when you *feel bad*," Latoya said.

"Exactly."

"Then why is my sentence wrong?"

I looked at her sentence again. She had written, *The man remorsed because he stole the money.* I understood what she had been trying to do. Instead of saying *The man felt bad because he stole the money*, she replaced *felt bad* with *remorse*. It was a common mistake.

"Let me show you this real quick," I said to Latoya, leaning over her paper. "Remorse is a noun, right? It's something you *feel*? Well, a better way to use the word would be 'The man *felt* remorse because he stole the money.' It's used like the word *courage*. What does courage mean?"

Latoya thought for a moment. "It's when you feel brave and strong."

"Okay. So would you say 'The man *couraged* before going into battle, or would you say 'The man *felt* courage before going into battle'?"

The light went on in her brain. "Oh, *right*," she said. "Now I get it. I used *remorse* as a verb and not a noun."

"Bingo."

Latoya went back to writing her sentences. I circulated the classroom, working several students through the same issues Latoya had. The atmosphere stayed positive. After the vocabulary, we read "The Sniper." It was about a man trying to shoot a sniper on a rooftop in Dublin during Ireland's war for independence against Great Britain. In the end, the man manages to kill the sniper, only to realize it was his brother. The students loved the story, especially the final twist.

The rest of the day was just as successful. I studied "The Sniper" with all of my classes and got positive responses. I began to realize that this year's freshmen class *was* a better, more respectful bunch and that my teaching and classroom management *was* improving.

A week later, when things continued to run smoothly, I started to believe I could make it through the year. By the beginning of October, I knew without a doubt. I was forming a relationship with my students, and we were establishing a mutual respect for each other. Last year's blunders began to fade, and little by little, I grew more confident. It was around this time that I actually got *satisfaction* from teaching, something I hadn't experienced in a long, long while.

THE SONG LYRICS PROJECT

As the holidays approached, I began to enjoy my students even more. My sense of humor had broken through, finally, and I was more relaxed in class. I still had my share of discipline problems, but I was learning how to defuse them, how to keep them from escalating into bigger issues. My instruction was also getting more creative. One week before the Christmas break, I introduced my song lyrics project, a lesson that used music to teach the elements of literature as well as figurative language. Students were required to get a copy of their favorite songs and transcribe the lyrics on paper. Next, they had to analyze the lyrics and try to identify one example of figurative language (simile, metaphor, hyperbole, or personification), identify one example of alliteration, find one symbol and explain what it symbolized, and as a conclusion, they had to write a 200-word interpretation of the song's theme.

I started the lesson by reviewing with the class examples of these literary elements. I started with simile, and explained that it was a comparison using the words "like," "as," or "than."

"Can anyone give us a simile?" I asked. "Okay, Tony?"

"It's hot as balls in this room," Tony said.

The class burst out laughing. I smiled and rolled with the punches.

"That's actually correct," I said, "although it's not appropriate to use that word in class. Let's try to be less vulgar and more creative. How about a metaphor? Remember, a metaphor is like a simile, only it doesn't use the word 'like,' 'as,' or 'than.'"

These were harder to grasp than similes; although, on the surface they seemed easy. Metaphors had subtleties that were sometimes hard to identify. To help my students create metaphors, I first had them write a simile and then remove the *like* or *as* from it. For example, I had them write the simile *The man was as strong as an ox* and then rewrite it to say *The man was an ox*. There you had it—instant metaphor.

A boy named Ray raised his hand. He was African American and mildly autistic. At 15, he was 6 feet tall, 200 pounds. He had thick stubble on his cheeks and neck, and if he ever went into a bar, he'd get served alcohol without an ID. But his mature intimidating presence was underscored by his autism. When he spoke, he was timid, like a child. Some of the other teachers lovingly referred to him as a "gentle giant" because he was such as nice boy, so courteous and respectful. It seemed everyone had a soft spot in their heart for Ray, myself included. Ray was cool, a unique and meaningful personality in the class.

"Yes, Ray?" I said. "Do you have a metaphor you want to share with us?"

Ray thought for a moment, then he said, "The man was strong and tall."

I paused for a moment, smiled. "Okay, that's close, but here's the thing. A metaphor is a *comparison*, right? You need to be *comparing* two things. When you say 'The man is strong and tall,' what are you *comparing*?"

I could see the wheels turning in Ray's head. The answer was right on the tip of his brain.

I went over to his desk to help him. I modeled several more metaphors and explained that what he'd written was a *description*, not a comparison. I explained that he needed to *compare* the man to something for it to be a metaphor.

"The man was as big as a house!" he said triumphantly.

"You're *so* close," I said to him. "But what you just said was a simile. You used the word 'as'."

"Oh yeah," Ray said.

"That's fine. Just take out the word 'as,' and make it a metaphor."

"The man . . . the man *is* a house?"

"You got it," I told him and gave him a high-five. "The man is a house. Nice work, Ray."

Ray smiled proudly.

I went back to the lesson on figurative language. After I modeled all the definitions, I gave out a paper with the actual instructions for the song lyrics project. I explained that it would be two parts—written and oral. I reiterated that they needed to pick a song, write down the title, the artist, and lyrics, and then identify the literary elements. This needed to be typed, double-spaced, using 12-point font. If they didn't have access to a computer, they could hand write it neatly on a piece of looseleaf paper, but I wouldn't accept any papers ripped out of a notebook with the raggedy edges. They had to take pride in this assignment because it would be a major project grade.

This assignment was due in two days. I explained that at the start of class on Wednesday I was going to call a name at random and that person would have to come to the front of the class and present his or her paper. He or she would also need a copy of the song, either on CD, tape, or video, so they could play the first verse of it to the class.

Wednesday arrived, and to my satisfaction, the presentations went very smoothly. The students were enthusiastic and well prepared. Once in a while, a student would start chatting to a friend during a song, but they were quickly chided by a classmate to shut up and stop being so impolite. "There's someone presenting," they'd say. "Stop being so rude." My insistence on manners and common courtesy was actually rubbing off on them.

The diversity of the songs was impressive. It was clear most students put their *hearts* into it, that they'd put a great deal of effort into choosing their artists. To a lot of these teens, the presentation was a big deal. Their songs were a reflection of *them*—who they were and what they stood for.

Not all students went for popularity, and this is what impressed me the most. Many kids went for something more personal, more individual. An African American boy named Martin, who would in three years graduate from Swenson and become a United States Marine and eventually serve in Iraq, chose a gospel song, "Precious Lord," covered by Al Green.

When Martin hit play on the boom box on my desk and the power of Green's voice, along with the accompaniment of the backup choir, came across the speakers, I was moved. Moved by the music and moved by Martin's courage. Here was a young man standing in front of his peers playing *gospel* music, and he wasn't the slightest bit embarrassed or self-conscious. In fact, he was *proud*. I knew just how hard it could be to stand up in front of the class and open yourself to a bunch of teenagers, to let down your defense and show who you really were. Martin was doing so without flinching.

The first verse of the song ended, and Martin turned off the music.

"Amen, brother!" a kid in the back shouted. The class broke out laughing. But it was a *respectful* laugh, a sign of endearment and approval. It was a way to show Martin that he was all right with them. Martin smiled humbly.

"Great song," I said to Martin.

"Thanks."

"So, did you find any figurative language in the song?"

He explained that there were no similes or metaphors, and that there wasn't any personification or hyperbole either.

"Okay," I said, scanning through the lyrics of the song. "Did you find any symbolism?"

He looked at his paper. "Yes, I found some symbols," he said. "The lyrics about the 'storm' and the 'night' represent tough times in a person's life. These are times when you might have lost your way, or when you lost faith in God. The word 'light' is also a symbol. It represents salvation or the path where you want to be. It could also mean God or heaven."

"Excellent," I said. "Now can you finish by giving us your interpretation of the song?"

"Sure." Martin read his 200-word interpretation. In it, he explained that the song was about a person calling on God for help in tough times. He explained that no matter how lost you feel, that if you turn to the Lord, he will guide you. He also said that to him, the song was all about having faith. Those with faith can overcome anything. He gave personal examples to make his case.

"Great job," I said to Martin. I took his paper and started clapping. The class joined in with the applause.

"Thanks," Martin said. He smiled and sat down.

The rest of the presentations went just as smoothly. I was pleasantly shocked by the kids' focus and enthusiasm. Again, I was also impressed by the sheer diversity of the music. In addition to Martin's choice of gospel, there was hip-hop (Tupac Shakur), R&B (Boyz II Men), pop (Michael Jackson), love songs (Whitney Houston), heavy metal (Metallica), and classic rock (The Doors), among others. Interestingly, all the students listened to their peers' songs respectfully, tolerant of the diverse styles, genres, and cultures. That was the one thing I had always admired about Swenson's student body: they were color blind to each other and, for the most part, embraced multiculturalism and had interracial relationships. There was also no racial achievement gap at Swenson; PSSA tests revealed that whites did not outscore their fellow black and Latino counterparts.

Big Ray was the last student to present. Surprisingly, he graced our presence with a little bit of Guns N' Roses. The song he chose was "Welcome to the Jungle." I remember this vividly because of how well he grasped the concept of metaphor, which he had struggled with so much at the beginning of the week.

"The 'jungle' in the song is a metaphor," he told the class after he played the first verse of the song.

"Very good. Can you tell us why it's a metaphor?"

"Because the song's really about a big city or a place where you can get drugs and all kinds of bad things. The song is comparing a big city to a jungle."

"Right on the money," I said to Ray, impressed. He smiled. The class voiced their encouragement.

"Yeah, Ray!" a student called out.

After Ray gave his interpretation, he sat down. Things were starting to come together nicely. I stood at the front of the classroom, inspired and grateful.

TEN
Multiculturalism and the Achievement Gap

In July of 2010, the Educational Testing Service issued a policy information report titled *The White-Black Achievement Gap: When Progress Stopped*. The report, authored by Barton and Coley, traces America's racial achievement gap from the civil rights era to 2008. The report notes the gap had two periods: one of progress and one of stagnation. The period of progress ran through the 1970s and 1980s when the National Assessment of Educational Progress (NAEP) began collecting national data on student achievement. It was during this period that the white-black skills gap in reading and math was significantly narrowed and, in some cases, cut in half.[1] The period of stagnation began around the late 1980s, when the white-black gap leveled off and, in some cases, even began to widen.[2] The stagnation period was particularly troublesome because it affected those born around the late 1960s, a time when equal-rights legislation began putting an end to racial discrimination.

There are numerous theories as to why America's racial achievement gap continues to exist. One widely acknowledged source of the skill differential is educational equity. Research shows that minority students most in need of an education attend schools with the least qualified and least experienced teachers.[3] Studies also reveal that minority students are offered less challenging curriculum, have less access to technology in school, attend schools with high class size, and are more likely to report issues of fear and safety at school.[4]

According to *Yes We Can*, a 2010 report prepared by the Schott Foundation focusing on the education of black males in America, "the overwhelming majority of U.S. school districts and states are failing to make targeted investments to provide the core resources necessary to extend what works for Black male students. Thus, in the majority of U.S. states, districts, communities and schools, the conditions necessary for Black males to systemically succeed in education do not exist."[5]

Home environment is another possible source of the achievement gap. In Barton and Coley's 2009 report *Parsing the Achievement Gap II*, as mentioned previously, national trends between students of different racial and socioeconomic backgrounds were tracked. The report lists 16 factors that have been linked to student achievement. Of the 16 factors, nine were directly related to a child's home environment.[6]

The report concludes, among other things, that minority students changed schools more frequently than nonminorities, that there was a higher percentage of black infants born with low birth weight than white and Hispanic infants, that the likelihood of being exposed to environmental hazards, such as lead and mercury, was higher for minority and low-income children, that minority and low-income children were more likely to lack proper nutrition, that parents of minority children were less likely to read to their children, that black children watch more television than white children, that it was less likely for minority students to live with two parents, and that white students tended to grow more academically over the summer than minority students.[7]

Although the report also attributes the achievement gap to school inequity issues, Barton and Coley do recommend placing an emphasis on improving the involvement of parents. "Families . . . have a large responsibility to regulate use of the TV set, read to young children, see that they get to school, and support efforts to foster discipline and order in the schools," they conclude. "Ignoring the impact of a student's home circumstances will do nothing to help teachers and schools narrow achievement gaps."[8]

Clearly the most controversial attempt to explain the achievement gap is the theory that there exists a disparity in IQ between whites and blacks. In *The Bell Curve: Intelligence and Class Structure in American Life*, Harvard professor Richard J. Herrnstein and American Enterprise Institute resident fellow Charles Murray make such a claim.[9] Although the book was a *New York Times* bestseller, it initially sparked outrage among the public. Herrnstein and Murray were accused by some of practicing scientific racism, and *The Bell Curve* was challenged with several published rebuttals, one of which was titled, *Intelligence, Genes, and Success: Scientists Respond to "The Bell Curve,"* which questions the validity of Herrnstein and Murray's underlying statistical arguments.[10]

Reactions to *The Bell Curve* did not end there. In 2003, California Newsreel, a video-production outfit and distributor dedicated to social change, released a three-part video series titled, *Race: The Power of an Illusion*. The video, supported by PBS and taught in university multicultural-education classes, not only argues that disparities in IQ fail to exist between races but also that *race* itself does not exist.[11]

California Newsreel gave the following promotional description of the video series on its website: "*The Power of an Illusion* questions the very idea of race as biology, suggesting that a belief in race is no more sound than believing that the sun revolves around the earth."[12] Part three of the series, titled "The House We Live In," was summarized as follows: "This episode uncovers how race resides not in nature but in politics, economics and culture. It reveals how our social institutions 'make' race by disproportionately channeling resources, power, status and wealth to white people."[13]

Regardless of politics, closing the racial achievement gap will take considerable focus and effort. Americans must work together at all levels to find comprehensive, holistic solutions.

MULTICULTURAL EDUCATION

In the fall of 2008, after teaching in Philadelphia for 11 years, I decided to go back to school to get my master's degree in multicultural education. I enrolled in this major because I wanted to learn new methodologies that would broaden my teaching repertoire. I also wanted a crash course on world culture and some supplementary materials I could use to help diversify my lesson plans.

Surprisingly, as I completed the core courses in this major, I realized I was receiving almost none of this. What I did get was politics—one-sided ideologies that had little to do with education or teaching strategies. These ideologies, as explained by various professors in the program, were supposed to open my mind and make me more tolerant of diversity. Ironically, after taking the class Multicultural Education, I found myself not becoming more open minded but just the opposite: I found myself getting frustrated and becoming less patient around the high school students I taught back at Swenson.

The required reading for Multicultural Education was as follows:

1. *Why Are All the Black Kids Sitting Together in the Cafeteria?* by Beverly Daniel Tatum. An underlying premise of this book is that whites in America had a "privilege" that was systematically denied blacks. In addition, the text talks about "institutional racism," and how whites were guilty of this simply because they existed inside a "privileged" society. The book also lobbies for affirmative action and suggests that anyone who opposes it is an "aversive racist."
2. *A Different Mirror: A History of Multicultural America* by Ronald Takaki. This book was quite interesting but was also quite antiestablishment. The author focuses on information that highlights America's sinful past—all the ways society and government mistreated immigrants and people of color.

3. *We Can't Teach What We Don't Know: White Teachers, Multicultural Schools* by Gary R. Howard. This book discusses "Western white dominance" and how to put an end to it through education. It suggests, among other things, that the racial achievement gap in America is the fault of white teachers who didn't embrace or strive to understand their students of color.
4. *Cultural Diversity and Education: Foundations, Curriculum, and Teaching* by James A. Banks. This book is the most objective of the four. It gives a history of multicultural education and thoroughly explaines the movement's principles, ideologies, and foundations.

Needless to say, I was taken aback when I began the reading. What disappointed me wasn't that the course was rooted in politics and had little to do with practical, hands-on teaching strategies or methodologies. The frustrating part was that the course was so *one sided*.

Once during class, after hearing the professor lecture on white-flight in large American cities in the 1940s and 1950s, I questioned the idea that deteriorating conditions in urban areas were the result of the G.I. Bill and a racist white society.

"What percentage of urban blight has to do with bad personal decisions?"

The professor looked at me like I had blasphemed. "What are you saying, Chris?"

I repeated my question in a very respectful manner and explained that I was simply trying to look at all sides of the issue and think outside the box.

"We're not going to talk about *that*, Chris," the professor said with a tone. "We're focusing on white racism and the G.I. Bill." And that was it. End of conversation. The professor moved to the next topic, never bothering to answer my question.

I remember leaving the class fuming. I felt marginalized, like my viewpoints were somehow inferior or taboo. The irony was that this master's level course was the total antithesis of the high school English classes I ran at Swenson. I too held debates and discussions on race with my students (who were evenly mixed between black, white, and Latino), but regardless of my opinion on the matter, I *never* shut down a student and refused to answer his or her question. In fact, my own opinion never came out in the debate; I wanted to let my students work the issues out for themselves. Unlike my multicultural education class, I left the floor open for *all* points of view.

The irony (or hypocrisy) of the multicultural education class was that the professor wasn't truly interested in free thought. It was clear that he had already prescribed a method of thinking that he wanted the class to follow, and he actually graded you on how well you accepted that line of thought. He had an interesting word for adopting this thought: he called it your "growth."

Tragically, this "growth" was having a very negative effect on me. I was slowly becoming resentful, and I had to make a conscious effort not to allow this to affect my teaching. For years, I'd treated my students as *students*, color blind to their skin tone, but now race and all of its negative energy was creeping into my thinking throughout the day: *this kid's probably doing this because he's black; this kid's probably doing this because he's white; this kid has a "privilege," this kid doesn't*. It was maddening.

When the class finally ended, it took me a whole month before I saw the high school students I taught simply as *students* again.

THE SOCIAL JUSTICE MOVEMENT

On October 22, 2009, U.S. Secretary of Education Arne Duncan gave a speech at Columbia University's Teachers College about reforming the teaching profession:

> I believe that education is the civil rights issue of our generation. And if you care about promoting opportunity and reducing inequality, about promoting civic knowledge and participation, the classroom is the place to start. Children today in our neediest schools are more likely to have the least qualified teachers. And that is why great teaching is about more than education—it is a daily fight for social justice.[14]

The term "social justice," the 21st-century buzz-phrase for equal rights, has found a permanent place in the American lexicon. The term has acquired a certain trendiness to it; although its meaning can at times be nebulous and vague. The website BusinessDictionary.com provides a good definition of the term: social justice is "fair and proper administration of laws conforming to the natural law that all persons, irrespective of ethnic origin, gender, possessions, race, religion, etc., are to be treated equally and without prejudice."[15]

Most Americans would agree that this is a pretty accurate definition of social justice. Obviously, based on outside factors such as politics, religion, and social class, the concept of social justice will vary slightly from person to person and group to group. However, no one is going to argue its main premise: the need for fairness and equality in society.

Social justice in schools—the premise that educational equity will ultimately bring about an end to bias, discrimination, and the devastating effects of the achievement gap—is based on such a premise. Advocates of social justice believe that achieving this goal is of the utmost urgency. It is an active process; hence, the word *fight* used by Secretary Duncan. Social justice is a *cause*, a *mission*, a *struggle*. It's something that should be strived for and demanded daily. Most would agree that civil rights and equality are indeed worthy of a conscious effort and fight.

However, it is in the implementation of social justice—the means behind *bringing about* fairness and equality—where ideals clash and things start to get a little messy. This is especially the case when it comes to public schools. In an attempt to bring "balance" to education, practitioners of social justice sometimes adopt an antiestablishment mentality, an attitude that can serve to build walls rather than tear them down.

Sandra Stotsky, education professor and former senior associate commissioner at the Massachusetts Department of Education, writes about social justice and school curriculum in a 2008 article titled, "The Negative Influence of Education Schools on K–12 Curriculum":

> A "social justice" approach to teaching and learning, assumes that motivation to learn is enhanced by developing students' awareness of the historical and current grievances that social groups considered "oppressed" should hold against those who are to be perceived as their "oppressors." According to this theory, teachers should discredit traditional curricula and choose alternative curricula.[16]

She explains that, in some cases, such curricula is anti-civic, anti-Christian, anti-family, and anti-marriage. "White Americans tend to be portrayed as ugly racists in both fiction and nonfiction," she writes.[17] She also notes: "Many selections facilitate a stereotype of Christians in particular as hypocrites or bigots."[18]

Tragically, the divisive effect of such practices within the social justice movement is for the most part unacknowledged. Too many folks fighting for a "level playing field" seem to have adopted the idea that the end ultimately justifies the means. In fact, when it comes to higher education—especially the training of America's teachers—acknowledging that some aspects of "social justice" are harmful and polarize the races is met with resistance. As Rita Kramer writes in *Ed School Follies*:

> Any criticism of this state of affairs is met with the charge of elitism or, worse still, racism. No one in the ed school universe dares publically to advocate a curriculum that resists the "cooperative learning," the "multicultural" and "global" approach that is often a thinly disguised rejection of individualistic democratic values and institutions and of the very idea that underneath all our variety of backgrounds we Americans have been and should continue to become one nation, one culture.[19]

Beverly Daniel Tatum, president of Spelman College, explains in her book *Why Are All the Black Kids Sitting Together in the Cafeteria?* that there is a name for open-minded people who challenge or question multicultural policies aimed at social change such as affirmative action: they are called "aversive racists."[20]

There's no denying America's past sins. There's no denying certain groups have been exploited and victimized and continue to be today. However, as Dr. Martin Luther King Jr. would have advocated, you remedy hate with love, not with more hate. Stereotyping those who stereotype is not the answer. Striving for equal opportunity in society is indeed an admirable goal, but doing so through guilt and stigmatization is counterproductive and no viable way to close the achievement gap.

CULTURAL PLURALISM VERSUS ASSIMILATION

This is America. When ordering, please speak English.[21]

By now, we know the story. Joey Vento, owner of the famous Geno's Steaks in South Philadelphia, placed a small sign in the window of his restaurant asking customers to order in English. Although the Philadelphia Commission on Human Relations filed a discrimination complaint against Geno's (which the commission eventually lost), Vento said the sign was never meant to be offensive.

"This country is a melting pot, but what makes it work is the English language," Vento told members of the commission.[22]

How we react to this "speak English" sign says a lot about who we are and what we believe in. Those who find it offensive are probably cultural pluralists. Those who agree with its message are most likely assimilationists.

If you're not familiar with these concepts, allow me to elaborate on their meanings.

According to James A. Banks, author of *Cultural Diversity and Education*, "It is extremely important, argues the pluralist, for individuals to develop a commitment to their culture and ethnic group, especially if that group is oppressed by more powerful groups within society.... Each member of a culture or ethnic group has a moral obligation to join the liberation struggle."[23]

In other words, cultural pluralists believe you should not only be permitted to speak in your native tongue, but you should do it with pride and resist anyone or anything that tells you otherwise.

On the other hand, according to Banks, assimilationists believe the following:

> Strong ethnic attachments are dysfunctional in a modernized civic community. The assimilationist sees integration as a societal goal in a modernized state, not ethnic segregation or separation. The assimilationist thinks that the best way to promote the goals of society and to develop commitments to democratic ideals is to promote the full socialization of all individuals and groups into the shared national civic culture.[24]

In other words: *This is America. When ordering, speak English.*

Today, the debate between cultural pluralism and assimilation isn't limited to cheesesteak shops in South Philly. America's schools are jumping into the fray as well. Educational policy makers and those interested in school reform are battling over ideas and curriculum in regard to multicultural education. And like the heated debate over Vento's sign, each camp has a set agenda and interprets research very differently.

When it comes to education, the pluralist believes that the cultures of ethnic groups are not deviant or deficient in any way but are well ordered and highly structured—although different from the dominant culture. To quote Banks, pluralists believe "curriculum should be revised to reflect the cognitive styles, cultural history, and experiences of cultural groups, especially students of color."[25]

Educational assimilationists believe that learning characteristics are universal across cultures and that the socialization practices of the dominant culture enhances learning, while the socialization styles of ethnic groups hold their members back from succeeding in school. "Emphasis should be on the shared culture within the nation-state because all citizens must learn to participate in a civic culture that requires universal skills and competencies," Banks writes of the beliefs of assimilationists.[26]

Both the cultural pluralist and assimilationist concepts have their drawbacks. The pluralist theory is lacking because it often fails to prepare students to cope adequately with the real world beyond their ethnic or cultural community. And because learning characteristics are not always universalistic, but to some extent, cultural specific, the assimilationist theory is not completely foolproof.

The answer to curriculum reform is what Banks calls "multicultural ideology." Banks states, "Educational policy can best be guided by an eclectic ideology that reflects both the cultural pluralist position and the assimilation position, but avoids their extremes."[27]

In other words, we need educational policies that promote social cohesion and a minimum of mainstream socialization, but at the same time, take into consideration a student's learning style based on his or her culture or ethnic background.

CELEBRATION DOESN'T MEAN CONFRONTATION

In February of 2006, during Black History Month, the *Philadelphia Inquirer* published an educational supplement in its newspaper called "22nd Annual Celebration of Black Writing."[28] The supplement featured several African American and Latino writers, one of whom was Amiri Baraka, the militant writer who was removed as New Jersey's poet laureate in 2002 because of his inflammatory poem about the 9/11 terrorist attacks called "Somebody Blew Up America."

Looking for material to incorporate into my English classes, I took a closer look at the supplement. The section dedicated to Baraka had provided a link to his website and explained that it regularly published new information. I visited the website and, stunned, found it was a platform for racially charged rhetoric about riots and revolution.

Concerned about the appropriateness of this content, I sat down and wrote a commentary about the inclusion of Baraka in an educational supplement created for schoolchildren. A week later, my article was published in the *Philadelphia City Paper* under the headline "Here's a Radical Idea: Keep Amiri Baraka out of English 101." The article recapped my issue with Baraka:

> Then I visited his Web site, www.amiribaraka.com, for background information. The material I found there was quite shocking. On the first page was an article, apparently by Baraka, headlined, "Does Newark Want to Go Back to 1967?" The article went on to talk about the race riots in the cities of Detroit and Watts in the 1960s (Baraka called them "rebellions"), and how Blacks in New Jersey must continue to stand up against the "racist repression" of the White power structure in America.[29]

I go on to conclude that editors of such black writing supplements should choose authors who promote celebration—such as Eric Jerome Dickey, Terry McMillan, Toni Morrison, or Alice Walker—and not confrontation.

The reaction I received from the article was surprising. The *City Paper* was flooded with mail, and for two consecutive weeks, they printed letters from readers responding to my article.[30] Nearly all of them came from the same perspective: I was out of line for suggesting that Baraka should be removed from the supplement. One woman in particular wrote that racism was far from over and that children needed to hear Baraka's voice. She felt students had every right to be angry, that this anger should be embraced, not dismissed.

After reading the letters, I wondered about one thing in particular: how was this a *celebration*? How was ripping open old wounds from the 1960s and priming our city's children to be angry and standoffish helping education? How was it helping them love their neighbor? More importantly, how was this helping race relations and tolerance for diversity?

A week after my article ran in the paper, I received a message in my mailbox at Swenson that an organization of black journalists had called asking to speak with me regarding my commentary. I looked at the message and noticed that it had a New Jersey area code; Amiri Baraka was from New Jersey. Refusing to back down from what I'd written (but wanting to be open-minded and communicate), I called the number on the slip of paper. No one answered, so I left a message. I explained who I was and that I was interested in hearing what they had to say about my article. I asked them to return my call at Swenson so we could have a discussion.

In the end, no one got back to me. However, about six months later, I was surfing the Internet and happened to notice that Amiri Baraka had completely redesigned his website. Gone from the home page was the militant rhetoric and images, and in its place was a picture of a more mature Baraka standing at a microphone in round glasses and a straw hat, manuscripts of poems in hand.

Although I don't know for sure, I like to think I had something to do with this change of image.

There is a time and a place for confrontation, but when it comes to diversity and multiculturalism in America's schools, compassion should be stressed over aggression. We must continue to work for educational equity, but we must be careful not to antagonize and polarize the races in the process.

THE MIDDLE WAY

"Nationwide, more than 35 percent of public school students are Hispanic or Black, but less than 15 percent of our teachers are Black or Latino," Secretary Duncan told an audience of future teachers in 2009 at Columbia University. "That's a problem that is not self-correcting—we must proactively work on it. It is especially troubling that less than two percent of our nation's teachers are African American males."[31]

Secretary Duncan's choice of words are quite curious: "That's a problem that's *not self-correcting.*" Like the shortage of minority teachers in schools, there have been numerous suggestions for closing the academic achievement gap among American students. Regardless of particulars, each solution falls into one of two categories: *intrinsic* and *extrinsic*.

An intrinsic solution aimed at closing the achievement gap is a bottom-up approach and consists of one internal variable: the student *himself* or *herself* (this also includes the parent when dealing with elementary children). An extrinsic approach to fight the skills gap is a top-down method and consists of a multitude of outside variables, such as teachers, schools, counselors, budgets, educational policies, social programs and politics, the government, just to name a few. An intrinsic approach is based on self-empowerment, while an extrinsic approach is often rooted in the notion of powerlessness and oppression. The former believes that schools are an extension of communities; the latter argues that communities are an extension of schools.

Progressives in charge of reforming education have been trying to close the achievement gap *extrinsically* for many years. In other words, they argue it's the *system*—not the *individual*—that holds the key to success. In the Schott report, Michael Holzman states this fact point blank:

"In addressing this critical problem, it's essential to note that Black male students do not do poorly in all states, districts, communities and schools; if they did, the solutions to their achievement gaps might plausibly focus on the students themselves."[32] In one simple sentence, Holzman absolves the individual of the fundamental responsibility for acquiring an education.

Interestingly, there are six common arguments made by education advocates to explain the racial achievement gap in the United States:

1. Minority students fail academically because their teachers have low expectations.
2. Minority students are frequently mislabeled as learning disabled and emotionally disturbed because of misdiagnoses by teachers and counselors.
3. Minority students are passed over for gifted and advanced placement programs because of an unconscious racial bias.
4. Minority students are often disciplined inappropriately and expelled from schools because of prejudice or a misunderstanding of their culture.
5. Minority students dropout because they are "pushed out" by districts and uncaring teachers.
6. Minority students do not graduate because the education system fails to provide them with special supports.

These arguments, however valid, are noteworthy for one reason: all six center on *extrinsic* factors. None stems from the individual but from outside variables.

Although trying to close the achievement gap through efforts to restructure the public school system around the specific needs of minority students is an admirable goal, it's limited. Why? Because the academic achievement of minority students ultimately rests on *someone else's* watch; these children (and parents) have not truly become empowered and have not wholly taken responsibility for their education.

There is no question all students can achieve. There is also no question that the achievement gap in America stems from both past and present educational inequities. However, current solutions are often too focused on extrinsic variables. In short, there needs to be a *middle way*—a better balance between solutions based on the external "system" and solutions that focus on an internal paradigm shift within the individual and his or her family.

In my 14 years teaching in the Philadelphia School District, I've taught hundreds of minority students. These children have not only made me proud to be a teacher, but also many have outperformed their white counterparts. However, they were not perfect. In every case, there was plenty of room to improve.

When it comes to closing the achievement gap, why not meet halfway? While we demand an improvement in teacher quality, why not call for an improvement in student work ethic? While asking counselors to be more sensitive to a student's cultural differences, why not reinforce the need for positive, respectful behavior? While fighting for better schools, why not explore extracurricular learning options? In the information age, there is an unlimited amount of educational material in libraries and online to supplement lessons taught by "mediocre" teachers in low performing schools.

Although these suggestions are both fair and practical, they will undoubtedly be met with objections from urban education advocates. These groups might argue that the intrinsic change I mention is unrealistic because educational inequities are keeping minority children and their families out of the very system I am calling on them to engage in. They might argue that too many urban school systems do not include educational "stakeholders"—those students, parents, and community members who have the most to gain or lose at the hands of the school system—in the process of making decisions regarding school programs and district policy.

This is a reasonable argument. However, it is important for families to realize that in order to be a true *stakeholder*, you must first make an *investment*. People and institutions are not stakeholders by default or by birthright. In other words, to have a voice, you must *contribute*. This doesn't necessarily mean chairing school board meetings or running for the president of the PTA. Parents and community members bogged down by jobs or overwhelmed with other social ills can start small. They can bring baked goods to sporting events, chaperone field trips, or simply set academic ground rules in the home, such as implementing a nightly homework schedule or encouraging reading. These are good ways of claiming your stake, of putting your own sweat into the system.

Contrary to public perception, the student and the system are not *separate*. The student isn't *in here* and the system *out there*. All of us, the student, family, teacher, school, and community, *are* the system. Once we accept this reality, intrinsic solutions will meet halfway with extrinsic solutions, and finally all boundaries will be removed.

NOTES

1. Paul E. Barton and Richard J. Coley, *The Black-White Achievement Gap: When Progress Stopped* (Princeton, NJ: Educational Testing Service, July, 2010), 21, http://ets.org/Media/Research/pdf/PICBWGAP.pdf

2. Barton and Coley, *The Black-White Achievement Gap*, 2.

3. Paul E. Barton and Richard J. Coley, *Parsing the Achievement Gap II*, (Princeton, NJ: Educational Testing Service, April, 2009), 13, www.ets.org/Media/Research/pdf/PICPARSINGII.pdf

4. Barton and Coley, *Parsing the Achievement Gap II*, 9, 15–17.
5. Michael Holzman, *Yes We Can: The Schott 50 State Report on Public Education and Black Males* (Cambridge, MA: Scott Foundation, 2010), 4, www.blackboysreport.org/bbreport.pdf.
6. Barton and Coley, *Parsing the Achievement Gap II*, 3–4.
7. Barton and Coley, *Parsing the Achievement Gap II*, 3–4.
8. Barton and Coley, *Parsing the Achievement Gap II*, 33.
9. Richard J. Herrnstein and Charles Murray, *The Bell Curve: Intelligence and Class Structure in American Life* (New York: Free Press, 1994), 276–77.
10. Bernie Devlin, Stephen E. Fienberg, Daniel P. Resnick, and Kathryn Roeder, *Intelligence, Genes, and Success: Scientists Respond to "The Bell Curve"* (New York: Copernicus, 1997).
11. California Newsreel, *Race: The Power of an Illusion*, 2003.
12. California Newsreel, www.newsreel.org/nav/title.asp?tc=CN0149 (accessed September 17, 2010).
13. California Newsreel, www.newsreel.org/nav/title.asp?tc=CN0149.
14. Arne Duncan, "Teacher Preparation: Reforming the Uncertain Profession" (remarks, Teachers College, Columbia University, New York, October 22, 2009), U.S. Department of Education, www.ed.gov/news/speeches/teacher-preparation-reforming-uncertain-profession.
15. BusinessDictionary.com, "Social Justice," www.businessdictionary.com/definition/social-justice.html (accessed September 20, 2010).
16. Sandra Stotsky, "The Negative Influence of Education Schools on K–12 Curriculum," National Association of Scholars, June 30, 2008, www.nas.org/polArticles.cfm?Doc_Id=229.
17. Stotsky, "The Negative Influence of Education Schools on K–12 Curriculum."
18. Stotsky, "The Negative Influence of Education Schools on K–12 Curriculum."
19. Rita Kramer, *Ed School Follies: The Miseducation of America's Teachers* (Lincoln, NE: iUniverse, 2000), 211.
20. Beverly Daniel Tatum, *Why Are All the Black Kids Sitting Together in the Cafeteria?* (New York: Basic Books, 2003), 118.
21. Associated Press, "Philadelphia Cheesesteak Shop Owner Defends 'Order in English' Policy," FoxNews.com, December 15, 2007, www.foxnews.com/story/0,2933,316939,00.html.
22. Associated Press, "Philadelphia Cheesesteak Shop Owner."
23. James A. Banks, *Cultural Diversity and Education: Foundations, Curriculum, and Teaching*, 5th ed. (Boston, MA: Pearson Education, 2006), 113.
24. Banks, *Cultural Diversity and Education*, 115.
25. Banks, *Cultural Diversity and Education*, 114.
26. Banks, *Cultural Diversity and Education*, 116.
27. Banks, *Cultural Diversity and Education*, 127.
28. Educational Supplement, "22nd Annual Celebration of Black Writing," *Philadelphia Inquirer*, February 1, 2006.
29. Christopher Paslay, "Here's a Radical Idea," *Philadelphia City Paper*, February 23–March 1, 2006.
30. Letters to the Editor, "Radical, But Necessary," *Philadelphia City Paper*, March 2–8, 2006.
31. Duncan, "Teacher Preparation."
32. Holzman, *Yes We Can*, 6.

ELEVEN
Teaching Shakespeare

In April of 1999, I taught my first Shakespeare play. The experience was bittersweet—a pleasure in terms of morale and student enthusiasm but challenging when it came to instruction. Not all my students were passing the quizzes and completing their assignments. It was starting to become clear that my students on lower reading levels were having difficulty comprehending the plot and analyzing some of the play's deeper themes. The same problem was happening with a student named Carlos, who spoke English as a second language, and a young lady named Mindy, who had a learning disability in reading and was mainstreamed into my English class.

I spoke with Dianne Kennedy, the English department head, about this problem, and she explained to me that I needed to differentiate my instruction to fit the needs of all the varying ability levels of students in my class. I explained to her that I probably had kids on at least *four* different reading levels in the class, and this didn't include Carlos, who struggled to even write a complete sentence in English, and Mindy, who was a special education student with an individualized education plan because she had trouble comprehending new vocabulary.

"This is insanity," I told her, frustrated. "I can't rewrite my lessons five times every day for every kid in the class."

She shook her head. "You don't have to write five different lessons," she told me. "Just differentiate your instruction on two or three broad levels. Take an activity, and try to design it to give the kids more than one way of completing it. Give them *choices*."

"For every activity?"

"Not *every* activity, but for the important ones. The key lessons in the unit."

"What about the other stuff?" I asked. "What about when we read the play? What do I do when the kids aren't able to understand the plot and the characters?"

"You need to break it down for them," she told me.

I nodded. "I *do* break it down. I break it down after every scene. Most of the kids in the class get it, but not everyone. Carlos and Mindy are having a lot of trouble. So are some of the other lower-level readers."

"Maybe you should slow down your pace," Dianne told me. "Sometimes doing less is more."

I thought about this for a moment but realized there was a problem with this as well. There were a group of advanced readers in the class who were already frustrated by what they considered a *slow* pace. These five or six students, very articulate writers and speakers, always finished the activities ahead of the class and always sat at their desks looking bored and unchallenged, like I was wasting their time by repeating everything a thousand times; it was *these* students who I felt the most guilty about.

I explained this to Dianne, and she just shrugged. "All you can do is your best," she told me. "Let the advanced readers venture ahead, go at their own pace. Focus on the struggling students. If Carlos is still having trouble speaking English, send him over to the ESL teacher in room 308. He's entitled to these services. The same thing for Mindy, your special education student. Send her to the resource room with Ms. Barnett. She can help Mindy go over some of the new vocabulary and maybe help with comprehending the text of the play. Also, try putting the students into groups. Put Mindy and Carlos in groups with stronger readers so they can help them get through the material."

"Okay," I said. "Thanks."

I followed Dianne's advice. I worked with the ESL teacher in 308 to help get Carlos up to speed speaking English, and I sent Mindy to the special education resource room for extra help with Ms. Barnett. These services, unfortunately, were only available part-time. The ESL teacher worked in another school in the afternoons and was only at Swenson for a half-day. Ms. Barnett's time was also limited. In addition to running the resource room, she taught a full load of special education classes herself.

To give Mindy and Carlos extra help inside the classroom, I did cooperative learning activities like Dianne had also suggested. I paired Mindy and Carlos with stronger readers so they could help them through the activities and the text of the play. As time went by, however, not much improved with Carlos's English or Mindy's ability to understand Shakespeare. I realized this one day when I had the kids do a translation exercise, where they had to take 10 consecutive lines from *Romeo and Juliet* and rewrite them into "current" language. I used the classic balcony scene in act 2, scene 2 as an example:

> JULIET: O Romeo, Romeo! wherefore art thou Romeo?
> Deny thy father and refuse thy name;
> Or, if thou wilt not, be but sworn my love,
> And I'll no longer be a Capulet.

"Okay," I said to Mindy, working with her individually. "What is Juliet saying here?"

"She is calling out, looking for Romeo."

"Close," I said, "but not exactly. If you look at the footnotes at the bottom of the page, what does the word *wherefore* mean?"

Mindy checked the footnotes. "Oh, I see, *wherefore* means *why*."

"Right, the word means *why*. So what is Juliet saying here?"

"Why are you Romeo?" Mindy answered.

"That's right."

"But that doesn't make any sense."

"Actually, it does," I told her. "She's asking why he has to be Romeo, a Montague, the son of her father's enemy. She goes on to ask Romeo to get rid of the name Montague, or if he won't do that, to love her anyway, and she'll get rid of the name Capulet. That's what those four lines are saying." I wrote down the translation in her notebook:

> JULIET: Romeo, Romeo, why do you have to be a Montague?
> Deny your father and pick a new name;
> Or if you don't want to, swear you'll love me,
> And I'll change my name from Capulet.

"You see how it works?" I said.

Mindy shook her head. She didn't get it. Neither did Carlos.

The advanced students, on the other hand, *they* got it. They were finished with the 10-line translation and sitting bored in their desks, waiting for more work. I instructed them to help their group members or go ahead and translate another 10 lines for extra credit while they waited.

But my problems differentiating Shakespeare didn't end with *Romeo and Juliet*. Another day, when I covered the most popular of Shakespeare's 154 love sonnets, number 18, otherwise known as "Shall I Compare Thee to a Summer's Day," I again had an issue with the differing skill sets of diverse readers.

I handed out a copy of the sonnet to all the students and started by looking at the title, which simply read: "Sonnet XVIII."

"Shakespeare wrote 154 sonnets," I began. "But he didn't give a single one of them a title. When he died and publishers collected them, they were simply given numbers, kind of like the way public schools in New

York City are just given numbers. Now, here's the question: what serves as a poem's title if there isn't one? Michelle?"

"The first line," she said.

"Bingo. The first line. What's the first line of this poem?"

"'Shall I compare thee to a summer's day?'"

"Yes, so that's the unofficial title of the poem. That's what people know it as. But officially, it's titled 'Sonnet XVIII'. Who knows what number XVIII is?"

"Forty-eight," a boy said.

"Nope."

"Ninety-three!" another shouted.

"Wrong again. Don't they teach you guys Roman numerals anymore?"

"I know the answer," Martin said. "It's eighteen."

"Very good. Eighteen. Now does anyone want to volunteer to read the poem for us?"

Martin stepped up to the plate and read the sonnet. He did a very good job considering the poem's 400-year-old vocabulary. When Martin finished, I asked the class if anyone could tell us what the poem was about. Responses were mixed. To keep their attention, I explained that Shakespeare may have written this poem to another man.

"Shakespeare wrote this to another guy?" a girl in the front row named Julie asked. "No way."

"Way," I said.

A rumble came over the class.

"Shakespeare was gay!" a student in the back shouted.

"Maybe," I told him. "But we don't know for sure. Remember, he was married with three kids. But he *did* leave his wife in Stratford and go to London for 20 years. All we know is that of Shakespeare's 154 sonnets, half were written to a 'dark lady,' and half were written to a man. Perhaps the Earl of Southampton, who was his patron."

I continued analyzing the overall meaning of the sonnet. Earlier, I had explained that sonnets had two parts: the octave (the first eight lines) and the sestet (the last six lines). Traditionally in a sonnet, a problem is posed or a question is asked in the octave, and the answer or solution is given in the sestet. I asked the students to reread the sonnet to see if they could find a problem or question in the first eight lines. As a class, we decided that the question was in the first line: "Shall I compare thee to a summer's day?"

"Why does Shakespeare want to compare this person to a summer's day?"

"Because he's gay!" the same student said.

"Alright," I said, "enough with that. I'm being serious here. Shakespeare obviously wants to celebrate this person's beauty, wants to communicate and capture it in an image. But as you read on in the sonnet, he can't compare this person to a summer's day. Why not?"

"Because summer ends," Judy said.

"Exactly. Summer ends. How do we know this? What part of the poem tells us this?"

"Line four," Judy said. "'And summer's lease hath all too short a date.' That's the problem in the octave."

"Excellent. Does everyone see this?"

Some of the students got it. Some didn't. Carlos and Mindy were completely lost.

"So what is the solution in the sestet? How does Shakespeare solve his problem of capturing this person's beauty forever?"

"By writing the poem," Judy said. "The last two lines in the sestet say it: 'So long as men can breathe or eyes can see, so long lives this, and this gives life to thee.' Right there. That's the solution. The sonnet itself."

"Right again. And did it work? Has the poem given this person eternal life?"

"Sure it worked," Judy said. "We're still reading the sonnet four hundred years later, right? So this person's beauty has been captured forever. It's not that complicated."

"Wonderful," I said. "Does anybody have any questions?"

Mindy raised her hand.

"Yes?" I said.

"I don't get it, Mr. Paslay."

"Neither do I," Carlos whispered.

I walked over and directed both Mindy's and Carlos's group partners to work through the sonnet again with them while I moved to the next activity to keep the advanced readers occupied and on task. Carlos and Mindy's partners worked with them, but the two still had questions. I made a note of this and decided Shakespearean sonnets were not appropriate for struggling readers such as Carlos and Mindy. The next day, instead of making the two suffer through sonnets, I had them look at an encyclopedia article on the Globe Theatre and identify the main idea while the rest of the class underwent the challenging task of writing their own 14-line Shakespearean sonnets. To my disappointment, Carlos and Mindy struggled through the article as well, especially Carlos.

Frustrated, at the end of class, I went yet again to Dianne Kennedy to ask her for advice. After I explained the situation, Dianne told me that the encyclopedia article, like the sonnet, was still too difficult for Mindy and Carlos and that I should find more appropriate material. I should also make the material more "hands-on" and engaging, perhaps some kind of project that involved more creativity, such as drawing, cutting, or pasting.

"Maybe you could have them turn Shakespeare's sonnet into a rap song," she suggested.

I was confused. "And drawing a picture or writing a rap song is going to bring Mindy up to grade level in reading?" I said. "It's going to help Carlos speak English?"

"Just keep them *engaged*," Dianne told me. "Group work is the key. So is differentiating your instruction. Children learn differently today. Research shows this."

"*What research*?" I pressed.

"*District* research," she told me. "The people downtown writing the policy. They make the decisions, we don't. Just keep your instruction engaging and high interest. Keep it cooperative. Make it hands-on and differentiate."

"Okay," I said, turned, and left. As I went back into my classroom to rework my lessons, I still didn't know how my English class was ever going to get Carlos and Mindy to understand Shakespeare, let alone get them up to grade level in reading.

TWELVE
Policy Matters

As America changes linguistically, economically, culturally, and academically, so do the children within its public schools. In an effort to keep up with the diverse needs of students, education leaders have been pushing the use of something called *differentiated instruction*. Differentiated instruction is a teaching method that requires teachers to tailor instruction to the specific needs of individual students. In other words, teachers do not develop a "one-size-fits-all" lesson, rather, they take that day's material and produce multiple activities geared toward the learning styles and ability levels of all children in the classroom.

Differentiated instruction, when used properly, can be effective. It allows students to learn at their own pace so stronger children can forge ahead while the weaker ones can spend more time digesting material. The thing about differentiated instruction, however, is that it's *not* being used properly in all situations. In large urban districts, such as Philadelphia, differentiated instruction has slowly morphed into a "cure-all" for a wide range of academic issues.

If a student in class is a struggling reader, for example, teachers have been instructed by administrators to differentiate their material. Likewise, if a student is an advanced reader, teachers have been instructed to differentiate. If a student is several grade levels behind in vocabulary, or has a learning disability, or a physical disability, or an emotional problem, or has limited English proficiency, teachers have been instructed to differentiate their material to fit student needs.

Teachers must differentiate their lesson plans as well as their lessons. Technically, they must also differentiate their assessments—their tests, papers, projects, oral presentations, and so forth. And this is done for every subject at every level, with every child in every class. The experts, such as Carol Ann Tomlinson, may object and insist that this isn't true, that proper differentiated instruction doesn't work like this. They will explain that differentiated instruction is *broader* than this, that it's not broken up and applied to every single child, rather, to whole groups. They will argue that it's about a teacher simply being flexible in his or her approach to teaching and that differentiating material can be achieved simply by focusing on three elements of teaching: content, process, and products.

Maybe so. However, educational leaders and those who influence policy must be careful not to overuse this instructional method. Its effectiveness can only go so far. For students to make gains, especially those in urban settings with high class sizes and other socioeconomic disadvantages, teachers must be provided with needed supports. Differentiation cannot replace reading assistants when it comes to student literacy. It cannot replace English as second language (ESL) teachers when it comes to students with limited English proficiency. It cannot replace special education teachers when it comes to students with learning disabilities.

Unfortunately, in school districts like Philadelphia, differentiated instruction *is* being used as a replacement for these things. Why? Because it allows school districts to do *more* with *less*. Not that big districts have a choice in most cases. As mentioned previously, urban schools are now expected to take on the role of families, and doing so stretches resources thin. Instead of lowering class sizes or hiring additional reading specialists, or ESL teachers, or special education assistants, educational leaders can get more bang for their buck by packing students with varied needs and skill sets into one single classroom with one single teacher and mouthing the magic word: *differentiate*.

Often, this doesn't work out so well, as might be expected. The reality of the situation is that even the most skilled and experienced teachers cannot do all things for all children. In other words, if kids come into the classroom lacking basic language and academic skills and haven't put in the requisite practice needed to develop them—and schools don't supply the manpower—there will be giant gaps in learning.

An example of this is vocabulary. Studies show that a student needs, on average, 12 encounters with a new word to master that word.[1] Now let's just say that a student is three years behind grade level in reading because his vocabulary is short 1,000 words. Let's also say an English teacher is expected to differentiate her instruction to help get the student up to grade level in reading. On average, the struggling student will need a total of 12,000 exposures to new vocabulary to make the jump to a proficient reading level. When is this supposed to take place? During some differentiated reading group work? Where are the "man" hours being put in? Where is all the mileage? Sure, experts say differentiated instruction should be viewed as an "escalator" and not "stairs" (which means teachers should focus on gradual progress), but this wasn't the expectation implied in No Child Left Behind in 2010 when educational leaders and politicians insisted *all* children must be academically proficient and performing on grade level.

As a running coach, I often compare education to the sport of cross-country. In particular, I liken the skills and aptitude a student needs to read at grade level to the strength and endurance a high school athlete needs to adequately run a 5K cross-country course. Like literacy, a runner's strength and endurance are built over time and involve putting in the proper mileage. When athletes don't show up to meets in the proper shape, their times on the course are compromised. For example, suppose a runner is having trouble at home. Suppose, because of financial reasons, a runner is forced to work a part-time job and, therefore, cannot make every practice or go on his long Sunday training runs. Instead of running 25 miles a week, he only does 5. On race day, when he cramps up in the middle of the course and is reduced to walking up the steepest hill, spectators on the sidelines want to know why.

"What's wrong with the coach?" one of them may ask. "Look at his runner. He's walking on the course!"

Patiently, the coach might explain that Jason, the boy huffing and puffing up the hill, didn't put in his mileage for the week. He was too busy working a part-time job. The spectator, unfamiliar with the nuances of distance running, might assume the coach is making an excuse. "If the coach were competent," they might reason, "if he provided the proper supports during the practices the boy *did* attend after school, everything would be fine."

The coach understands the misconceptions held by most spectators, so he nods and smiles. He's been coaching cross-country for many years and understands that when it comes to endurance, *nothing* can replace mileage. Somehow, somewhere, the work has to be done. And the reality is, Jason can't make up the missed mileage by running an extra 15 miles one day during practice. It just doesn't work like that.

So goes literacy. Differentiating instruction can work only if it's used correctly and not as a replacement for other supports.

ACADEMIC TRACKING

The problems stemming from the abuse and overuse of differentiated instruction can be solved in one simple step: academic tracking. Academic tracking is the practice of grouping students into separate classes based on achievement, a policy embraced primarily by schools serving students from higher socioeconomic backgrounds.[2]

High poverty districts, on the other hand, are more likely to resist tracking.[3] The practice of using ability levels to place students into separate classes has been so criticized and attacked in large urban districts that simply suggesting the idea can spark cries of classism and even racial discrimination. Opponents of tracking argue that it perpetuates academic and socioeconomic inequity and is a contributing cause of America's racial achievement gap. Michael Holzman writes in a 2010 report on the public education of black males:

> Stacks of research reports have indicated for years that Black male students are not given the same opportunities to participate in classes offering enriched educational offerings. They are more frequently inappropriately removed from the general education classroom due to misclassifications by the Special Education policies and practices. They are punished more severely for the same infractions as their White peers. On average, more than twice as many White male students are given the extra resources of gifted and talented programs by their schools as Black male students. Advanced Placement classes enroll only token numbers of Black male students, despite The College Board urging that schools open these classes to all who may benefit.[4]

Opponents of academic tracking also argue that grouping students by ability level affects children's self-esteem and harms them, as President George W. Bush once said, through the soft bigotry of low expectations.

According to research provided in the Southeast Regional Education Board's development guidebook, *Literacy across the Curriculum: Setting and Implementing Goals for Grades Six through 12*:

> Differences in the quantity and quality of curricula affects the amount of student reading and literacy instruction in secondary schools. . . . Students in lower tracks experienced less instruction, read less text and were taught less "culturally valued" content. This produced lower expectations for student performance. These students were unlikely to move into higher tracks and were unable to learn the content necessary for postsecondary education.[5]

When it comes to academic tracking, researchers have drawn several important conclusions. One is that low-performing students fare slightly better in heterogeneously grouped classes as opposed to remedial programs; this finding clearly favors those opposed to tracking.[6] Another finding is that tracking has little effect on average achievement.[7] However, when it comes to producing high-achieving students, tracked schools outperform those that are untracked.[8] This discovery makes it easy to understand why large urban districts serving diverse groups of students have pushed so hard to "detrack" their schools: because they are primarily interested in closing the distribution of achievement, otherwise known as the achievement gap.

But closing the distribution of achievement isn't all positive in and of itself. Although abolishing remedial tracks might provide some benefit to low-achieving students, the absence of higher-level tracks is clearly harming advanced students and the gifted. "In the name of equity, gap closing, political correctness, and leaving no child behind, American education has been a bit too willing to neglect its higher-performing students and the school arrangements that best meet *their* needs," writes Tom Loveless in his 2009 report *Tracking and Detracking: High Achievers in Massachusetts Middle Schools*.[9]

A common solution proposed to keep high-achieving students on pace is to simply raise the bar for *all* students—to require a school's entire student body to take high-level academic courses. This strategy has been tested with less than stellar results; simply placing a student in an advanced class is *not* necessarily a recipe for success. Tom Loveless finds in one study that over a quarter of math students scoring in the bottom 10 percent on the National Assessment of Educational Progress (NAEP) were enrolled in advanced math courses in 2005.[10] Loveless warns that pushing high-level math courses on low-performing students could further endanger their chances of success.

Large urban school districts need not throw the baby out with the bathwater. In other words, instead of doing away with tracking altogether, why not push to broaden the cultural awareness of educators so they could, in turn, track more accurately? Why not provide counselors and special education instructors with extra professional development so they could avoid misdiagnosing or mislabeling students as something they are not? Why not ingrain in teachers the policy of setting high expectations for all, regardless of the academic level of the class being taught?

Doing so would not only benefit the lower-level students but would respect the needs of the advanced and gifted students as well. It would also relieve teachers of the impractical burden of trying to create multiple activities to fit multiple students on multiple grade levels all at the same time.

LEAST RESTRICTIVE ENVIRONMENT AND THE "STAY-PUT" PROVISION

The effort to protect the rights of handicapped children and students with disabilities has further complicated education policy in American public school classrooms. In particular, the federal law known as the Individuals with Disabilities Education Act (IDEA) has several statutory provisions that in some cases can tax the system and make discipline more challenging. Two provisions that directly impact on classroom management are "least-restrictive environment" and the "stay-put" provision for pending discipline cases.

Least-restrictive environment is the philosophy that children with disabilities should be taught in regular education classrooms whenever possible. According to the fourth edition of *American Public School Law*, "The objective is to give the disabled child the opportunity to socialize and interact with other nondisabled children and, further, to reduce as much as possible any formal education processes that would tend to stigmatize or differentiate the disabled child."[11]

The stay-put provision, according to *American Public School Law*, "prohibits school officials from unilaterally excluding a disabled student from the classroom for dangerous or disruptive conduct for an indeterminate period of time where conduct grows out of a disability."[12] In other words, because disabled students have a right to education under federal law, they cannot be expelled from school or removed from the classroom for long periods of time during discipline hearings if it can be shown that their violent or disruptive behavior stems from their disability. If schools *do* remove disabled children from the classroom, the school is responsible for providing the child with alternative accommodations.

Because alternative accommodations cost money and use up valuable resources, regular education classrooms in large urban districts are often home to students with behavioral and emotional issues, including anger management problems. Tragically, when students with such issues and disabilities act out in a violent or confrontational manner, schools with limited resources must deal with the problem in-house. This usually involves a brief suspension and discipline hearing, at which time, it may or may not be found that the behavior stemmed from the student's disability. If it is determined that the behavior is, in fact, related to the disability, the student's individualized education plan (IEP) is updated, and the student is either given an alternative placement or, if such resources are unavailable, sent back into the regular classroom.

Years ago, a student whom I taught pushed and verbally assaulted a teacher in another classroom down the hall from me. The student was immediately arrested by Philadelphia police and given a five-day out-of-school suspension by the principal. During his suspension, because this particular student was learning disabled and had an IEP, a meeting was held by the special education coordinator and all the boy's teachers to determine if the boy's confrontational actions were a manifestation of his disability. It was determined, after careful review, that this student's actions were *not* related to his disability, which had to do largely with literacy issues and not anger issues. Simply put, the boy's outburst was out of the ordinary and not consistent with his normal behavior and disability.

In the end, the boy was removed from the school and sent to an alternative placement. The curious part of the incident was that if the boy's outburst *had* been a common occurrence and part of a larger emotional disturbance, the odds are he would have been protected under special education law and would have had the right to stay in this school. Stated another way, the more regularly violent and confrontational a student with a disability is, the better the odds are he will be extended an invitation to stay in a traditional school environment.

This is a reality many unfamiliar with special education law and the daily workings of public schools can't comprehend. In 2008, the *Philadelphia Inquirer* wrote an editorial headlined "Education Interrupted," an article demanding that city schools "must do more to quickly remove troublemakers by expediting expulsion hearings and meting out strict discipline."[13] The article was written in response to the 1,048 "serious" disciplinary incidents reported in the Philadelphia School District in the first two months of the 2008–2009 school year. The sentiments expressed in the editorial were echoed at the time by many of Philadelphia's citizens: city schools needed to do more to crack down on disruptive students.

However, what many didn't understand was that the district couldn't crack down because doing so, in many cases, would have been *breaking the law*. All students are entitled to due process before being expelled. And there are even more hurdles to clear before administrators can kick out students with learning disabilities. On top of this, in 2010, the No Child Left Behind law used both suspensions and expulsions to determine a school's Adequate Yearly Progress rating, which further influenced school leaders' decisions when it came to keeping unruly students in the classroom.

In order for teachers to adequately do their jobs, either special education laws must be updated or amended, or more resources must be made available for alternative placements.

COOPERATIVE LEARNING VERSUS DIRECT INSTRUCTION

Children learn differently in the 21st century. This is a statement repeated often by progressive scholars and urban school leaders in American education. The statement reflects the fact that American students are *changing*, not only academically but also linguistically, demographically, socially, and even behaviorally. When school leaders say children *learn differently*, what they are really implying is that we need to change the way we educate students.

In particular, school leaders and policy writers have been pushing to change the way teachers teach—to revamp and modify their instructional methodologies and styles of practice. The push has specifically centered on changing direct instruction to cooperative learning. For those not familiar with these terms, *direct instruction* is the traditional teacher-centered method of teaching where information is disseminated from the instructor through lecture, note-taking, drills, and formal skill practice. *Cooperative learning*, on the other hand, is a more progressive student-centered form of learning where kids get in groups and interactively engage in hands-on activities and projects.

Current trends in American education, especially in urban education, have dictated that a teacher's instruction should center on cooperative learning. In the 21st century, learning is supposed to take place in groups, and there should be *physical activity*—kids moving and talking with moderate to high volumes of educational noise. There should also be some form of project incorporated in the lesson, perhaps a handicraft (drawing, cutting, or pasting) or a field experience (visiting a greenhouse or taking soil samples in a nearby field). These practices are all generally applauded as good forms of teaching.

Direct instruction, on the other hand, has been shunned as ineffective and outdated. Teacher-centered instruction, lessons that involve lecture, note-taking, drills, and other formal practices that require students to work individually in a quiet and clinical setting, has been labeled by school leaders as rigid, boring, and inadequate; the phrase "drill and kill" has evolved to suggest that forcing students to do academic drills will kill their motivation to learn. Direct instruction, progressive scholars insist, should be used sparingly and in small doses; it should only be used as a *support* to student-centered group instruction.

Older generation teachers who grew up learning via direct instruction and who started their careers using direct instruction often have a hard time shifting away from this style of teaching. Instruction to them is clean and organized—students sit quietly in their seats, listen to the teacher, take notes, and complete the lessons given to them. A good portion of the work may be drills and involve memorization. Discussion and higher order questioning are highly structured and must follow a strict set of rules. Much of the time, direct instruction involves extended periods of reading, writing, computations, and other, rather dry, academic practices, all of which students complete individually in a controlled classroom environment.

Which is why educators accustomed to this kind of teaching—and more importantly, this kind of classroom management—often take issue with abandoning their orderly routines for the looser, more flexible style of project-based cooperative learning. Cooperative learning can at first appear quite messy to older teachers. The idea of breaking down the rigid structure of direct instruction and allowing students to collaborate on projects and discuss new information among themselves may seem very much like chaos. After all, students are *students,* so how could they possibly be able to teach themselves and their peers?

But project-based cooperative learning, championed by school reformers such as Bill and Melinda Gates, can increase student interest and make learning more fun. Bess Keller writes in *Education Week*:

> Proponents see the method as helping to remedy a lack of "rigor and relevance" in high school coursework, which they believe contributes to the nation's dropout problem. . . . Project-based learning presents

> students with real-world problems that ideally can be solved only by application of the knowledge and skills that have been set for them to learn. Typically, students work in teams to meet explicit standards, just as adults do at work.[14]

Interestingly, studies show race plays a factor in the success rate of cooperative learning. In 2009, the peer-reviewed journal *Cognition and Instruction* published a report that African American students work better in collaborative groups than individually. The study reveals the opposite for white students: Caucasians did their best work individually.[15] The learning styles of the two races may indeed be why large urban school systems, such as Philadelphia's, populated mostly by minorities, push group work over direct instruction.

Cooperative learning, however, isn't without its critics. Opponents argue student-centered instruction that revolves around hands-on projects might be fun, but that doesn't necessarily make it effective. Some argue it's intellectually thin and lacking in content and focuses more on entertainment than on instruction. "The traditional, teacher-centered approach generally produced higher academic achievement than the progressive, student-centered approach," writes Harvard professor and noted scholar Jeanne Chall after analyzing research on the subject.[16]

In 2008, George K. Cunningham, former University of Louisville professor, wrote in a report for the John William Pope Center for Higher Education Policy that a student-centered approach to learning was having a negative impact on student achievement. He states that under a student-centered philosophy "it is regarded as bad practice for teachers to actually do much teaching. They are supposed to act as 'the guide on the side' rather than 'the sage on the stage.'"[17] He also points out that the student-centered approach "is markedly inferior to traditional, 'teacher-centered' pedagogy, particularly when it comes to teaching students important skills like reading and math. Most students do better if they are taught with traditional methods, such as 'direct instruction.'"[18]

According to Cunningham's policy report, direct instruction is more effective because it gives students the close supervision they need in order to maximize their learning. It also maximizes instructional time, structures classrooms in such a way that the teacher is in control, and allows for appropriate questioning techniques to be employed.

As was apparent during California's whole-language movement, a lack of direct instruction significantly hurt children's ability to read. The same held true with "new math." In the late 1980s, the National Council of Teachers of Mathematics (NCTM) established a set of more student-centered national standards to raise the bar of student achievement, especially the achievement of poor and minority students. However, these new math standards were not giving students the skills they needed to achieve academically. According to Cunningham:

In part, the new standards were designed to be more "student-centered." . . . A major purpose of the NCTM standards was the redefinition of mathematics as a way to correct social inequities. The authors of these standards asserted that traditional mathematics instruction was a vehicle for the perpetuation of socioeconomic privilege. They pointed out that math performance often functions as a gatekeeper, preventing students with poor math ability from advancing academically. . . . The authors of the NCTM standards wanted a math instruction curriculum that would allow all students to do high-level math without mastering "low-level" problem-solving skills. To achieve this goal, the 1989 NCTM math standards decoupled advanced math performance from the mastery of math fundamentals. They did this by eliminating traditional algorithms, or sequences of rules, for performing such mathematical operations as long division, multiplication, and dividing fractions. Instead of requiring students to learn these algorithms, students were given the opportunity to "discover" creative ways of finding the answers.[19]

Education Week writer Peter West explains that critics of traditional math believed that most teachers placed too much emphasis on rote memorization and that the reform math placed "an emphasis on reasoning to find the appropriate solution to a problem, rather than depending on teachers to provide answers."[20]

Interestingly, it was right around this time that the racial achievement gap in math in the United States stopped closing and even began to widen in some age groups.[21]

Direct instruction, of course, can only be effective under the proper learning conditions. For this traditional methodology to work, there must also be a traditional learning environment: one that is relatively quiet, controlled, and filled with students who have the focus and self-control to engage in activities that are primarily academic, such as reading and analyzing sizable pieces of text and calculating mathematic equations.

Unfortunately, in the 21st century, too many students are unable to adequately handle these tasks, especially in large urban cities. Urban classrooms are home to struggling English language learners and children with attention deficit problems and anger management issues—many of whom have no one at home to help reinforce newly learned skills and material. Because direct instruction isn't conducive to students with such issues, it behooves educational leaders to dismiss the methodology as old-fashioned and promote project-based cooperative learning.

Ironically, the same reformers who advocate group and project-based learning also call for high-stakes standardized testing, which measures not a child's ability to work in groups or socialize but focuses on a student's mastery of rigorous core academic subjects, such as reading, writing, science, and math. In other words, current policy demands that teachers' instructional methods focus on learning styles that are practical and "real world," yet tests required under laws such as No Child Left Behind fail to assess such skills.

Because teachers and schools are being held accountable for children's mastery of core academic subjects and because not all students' learning styles are conducive to a single method of teaching, school reformers should consider striking a better balance between cooperative learning and direct instruction and refrain from labeling either learning style "ineffectual" or "old-fashioned."

PERSONAL VERSUS SOCIAL RESPONSIBILITY

In addition to differentiated instruction and cooperative learning, school reformers have been pushing teaching strategies and curriculum that advocate social responsibility. In particular, the teaching of "social justice" has become more prevalent, especially in school districts with large populations of minority students. As mentioned previously in chapter 10, the idea of social justice can mean different things to different groups, and its definition at times can be vague.

"Social-justice lessons are rarely taken from textbooks," writes Kathleen Kennedy Manzo in a 2008 article in *Education Week*. "They generally reflect multiple perspectives, particularly those of disadvantaged groups; question government policies and actions; and incorporate content and activities that encourage students to share their own experiences and participate actively."[22]

Although teaching social justice can work on critical thinking and help students get active in the government, critics note that it is often short on academic content—language arts, math, science, and so forth. In fact, in some cases, the very premise of social justice itself is the *rejection of curriculum*. Sandra Stotsky writes about teaching social justice in a 2008 article:

> This theory is associated with a school of thought called "critical pedagogy." Its basic concepts were popularized by Paulo Freire in *Pedagogy for the Oppressed*, first published in 1970. A Brazilian educator, a Marxist, and judged one of the most influential educators of the 20th century, Freire denigrated traditional curriculum content as oppressive and the pedagogy that he associated with it as a "banking concept of education" in which teachers "deposit" this oppressive knowledge into the minds of passive students. . . . To implement his ideas, teachers seek to develop their students' political understandings and attitudes—hostility or resentment in students belonging to social groups to be considered "non-dominant," and guilt in students who are to be perceived as members of the "dominant" groups. Motivating this theory in part is the idea that the relatively lower academic achievement and social status of these non-dominant groups may be traced to a lack of motivation

for, or resistance to, the cultural content and pedagogy of a curriculum that was not originally designed for them—thereby an alien and oppressive curriculum.[23]

Stotsky's observations raise an important question about teaching social justice: if academic content is secondary or even taught to be actively rejected, where are students getting their content knowledge in classes that teach social justice? If the lesson isn't taken from the textbook, where are they learning all the literature, math, science, and history they will be tested on under high-stakes standardized assessments such as No Child Left Behind?

Lack of academic content aside, there is something else worth discussing about teaching social justice: its primary message is about *social* responsibility as opposed to *personal* responsibility. There is a fundamental difference between these two concepts. Generally speaking, social change is extrinsic and takes place *out in society*. Teachers inspire students to right social wrongs by rising up and challenging things *outside* themselves, such as laws, curriculum, district policy, government policy, racism, bigotry, and so forth.

Teaching about personal responsibility is a completely different philosophy. This kind of change takes place *within*. Unlike social change, it's not about the actions of the *other guy*, rather, the actions of *ourselves*. Personal change is much more powerful and important than social change. Why? *Because there is no social change without personal change.* Think about it. In order to have social change, someone, somewhere is going to have to make a personal paradigm shift. If everyone refused to change personally, if everyone blamed the other guy, there would *be* no social change.

Unfortunately in the 21st century, this message has for the most part been ignored in education. Unlike the attitude in many European countries, where schools and teachers are respected, Americans have developed an attitude of entitlement. Too many kids, conditioned by progressive educational policy, have adopted a passive approach to their educations. Too many students have the following attitude: *I have the right to an education, now come and educate me.*

In other words, they are not being taught to be an active part of their own schooling. They are not receiving the message that their education is ultimately their *own* responsibility and that if they fail to get one, the first person they must blame is *themselves*. Geoffrey Canada, founder and CEO of the Harlem Children's Zone, spoke about student responsibility with Anderson Cooper in a *60 Minutes* interview aired in December of 2009. Although Canada is a visionary who's transformed thousands of children's lives, he doesn't ultimately feel his kids—meaning the students in the Harlem Children's Zone program—are responsible for their own schooling.

"If my kids don't go to college, people who work for me are losing their jobs. And there's just no way around that," Canada said. "I will fire the teachers, I'll fire the after school workers, I'll fire the directors. Everybody understands that this thing is *our* job as the adult, and we're not going to hold the kids responsible."[24]

Unfortunately, the idea that students aren't responsible for their own education has trickled down into the drinking water. When kids drop out, it's the school's fault. When they cut class, it's because of a boring teacher. When they fail a test, it's because of somebody else's low expectations. When they are disciplined, it's because they were misunderstood. When they don't graduate, it's because the system failed them.

For education to ultimately succeed, the students *themselves* must get active in their own educations. First and foremost, they need to *show up* for school; if they don't even come in the front door, they will never learn the skills needed to succeed. In addition, they must come to school prepared with the proper materials; they must complete homework assignments and practice the skills prescribed to them by their teachers; they must respect school rules, themselves, and their teachers and classmates; they must accept the fact that the purpose of school is to be informed—not *entertained*—and that they must be prepared to come out of their comfort zones and expand their horizons; and they must be prepared to go the *extra* mile, to supplement their own schooling by keeping up to date on current events, by reading and analyzing the abundance of information in the world around them so they can be lifelong learners. This is how students can get active in their education.

Of course, getting active doesn't mean *activism*, a practice that has been pushed by progressive school reformers along with the teaching of social justice. Just like with social justice, the policy of promoting activism among students is centered on *extrinsic* change, not personal responsibility.

Student activism is quite popular in the 21st century. However, a closer examination of activism reveals something interesting: activism isn't really active, but *passive*. *Active* change, one would think, would involve the person *directly* changing the unwanted situation or circumstance. For example, if you are thirsty, you go get a drink. If you want to get in shape, you go to the gym. If you want to lower your cholesterol, you eat healthy foods. That's *active*.

Activism in the 21st century doesn't work like this. Getting "active" under the principles of social change works more like this: If you're thirsty, you rise up and call on someone to bring you a drink of water; if you want to get in shape, you circulate a petition to have a personal trainer come to your house with a treadmill and weights; if you have high cholesterol, you go on a march and demand fast food companies remove fat from their products.

When students learn about activism as it relates to social change, they're ultimately learning about how to become dependent on a middleman. And being dependent on a middleman can be quite oppressive. Why? Because you yourself are still not empowered. Your success depends on the middleman's success, and sometimes the middleman just flat out doesn't give a darn. Trying to change the middleman's attitude is admirable, but why wait for *him*? Why not cut out the middleman and take away all his power?

Besides the middleman, there's another thing to think about when it comes to teaching activism: do teenagers really need to learn about rebellion? Dissidence? Civil disobedience? Don't adolescents, by nature, have these areas covered already? Some might suggest teamwork, citizenship, and collaboration might be better skills to teach impressionable young people.

Teaching social responsibility is noble and has its place in education, but a more practical approach might be to teach students to become self-empowered. That's known as *personal* responsibility, and that's what's lacking in 21st-century education.

NOTES

1. Steven A. Stahl and William E. Nagy, *Teaching Word Meanings* (Mahwah, NJ: Lawrence Erlbaum Associates, 2006), 68.

2. Tom Loveless, *Tracking and Detracking: High Achievers in Massachusetts Middle Schools* (Washington DC: Thomas B. Fordham Institute, December 2009), 22, www.edexcellence.net/publications-issues/publications/tracking-and-detracking-high.html.

3. Loveless, *Tracking and Detracking*, 22.

4. Michael Holzman, *Yes We Can: The Schott 50 State Report on Public Education and Black Males* (Cambridge, MA: Scott Foundation, 2010), 4, www.blackboysreport.org/bbreport.pdf.

5. Southern Regional Education Board, *Literacy Across the Curriculum: Setting and Implementing Goals for Grades 6 through 12* (Atlanta, GA: SREB, 2003), 21.

6. Loveless, *Tracking and Detracking*, 11–14.

7. Loveless, *Tracking and Detracking*, 11–14.

8. Loveless, *Tracking and Detracking*, 11–14.

9. Loveless, *Tracking and Detracking*, 3–4.

10. Tom Loveless, *The 2008 Brown Center Report on American Education: How Well Are American Students Learning?* (Washington DC: Brookings Institution, January 2009), 23, www.brookings.edu/~/media/Files/rc/reports/2009/0225_education_loveless/0225_education_loveless.pdf.

11. Kern Alexander and M. David Alexander, *American Public School Law*, 4th ed. (Belmont, CA: Wadsworth, 1998), 414–15.

12. Alexander and Alexander, *American Public School Law*, 4:435.

13. Editorial, "Education Interrupted," *Philadelphia Inquirer*, December 29, 2008.

14. Bess Keller, "No Easy Project," *Education Week*, September 19, 2007, 21–23.

15. Debra Viadero, "Study Examines Cooperative-Learning Results by Race," *Education Week*, May 13, 2009, 22.

16. Jeanne Chall, *The Academic Achievement Challenge: What Really Works in the Classroom?* (New York: Guilford, 2000), 171.

17. George K. Cunningham, *University of North Carolina Education Schools: Helping or Hindering Potential Teacher?* (Raleigh, NC: John William Pope Center For Higher Education Policy, January 2008), iii, www.johnlocke.org/acrobat/pope_articles/cunninghameducationschools.pdf.

18. Cunningham, *University of North Carolina Education Schools*, iii.

19. Cunningham, *University of North Carolina Education Schools*, 5.

20. Peter West, "The New 'New Math'?" *Education Week*, May 10, 1995, 21–23.

21. Paul E. Barton and Richard J. Coley, *The Black-White Achievement Gap: When Progress Stopped* (Princeton, NJ: Educational Testing Service, July, 2010), 2, http://ets.org/Media/Research/pdf/PICBWGAP.pdf.

22. Kathleen Kennedy Manzo, "Election Renews Controversy over Social-Justice Teaching," *Education Week*, October 29, 2008, 12.

23. Sandra Stotsky, "The Negative Influence of Education Schools on K–12 Curriculum," National Association of Scholars, June 30, 2008, www.nas.org/polArticles.cfm?Doc_Id=229.

24. "The Harlem Children's Zone," *60 Minutes*, CBS News, December 6, 2009, www.cbsnews.com/video/watch/?id=5914322n.

THIRTEEN
Arrival

As I became more experienced teaching, as my lessons grew stronger and my instruction and classroom management got more consistent, I began to settle in as an educator. Swenson, like me, also started to come into its own. In 2000, Swenson officially broke away from Lincoln High School and became a "stand-alone" school. This gave Swenson its own budget and governing body and, ultimately, gave the school the resources and supports necessary to meet the needs of its new "all-inclusive" status.

A big key to Swenson's turnaround, aside from the leadership of the principal and the administration, was the change in its admissions process. As Swenson faculty formed a recruiting team and began working with middle school counselors to promote its programs to eighth graders, Swenson began requiring applicants to undergo an interview before being placed into a lottery for acceptance. In 2001, nearly 2,000 eighth graders applied to Swenson. Although Swenson accepted students with a C average, they didn't take students with unsatisfactory behavior or poor attendance.

In the spring semester of 2002, I was given the opportunity to teach journalism. A primary function of the class, which was open to all Swenson students interested in news writing and current events, was to produce the school newspaper. This was one of the first orders of business when the class began. The first week, I broke students into groups of three and asked them to brainstorm for possible names for the paper. Students began writing titles down on slips of paper, at which time I collected and read them aloud to the class and asked for feedback.

"Okay," I said. "How about the *Swenson Voice*?"

"Man, that's *corny*."

"How about the *Pulse*?"

"*Boo*," someone shouted.

Finally, after three days of discussion, an African American student named Lawrence came up with the *Swenson Scroll*, a title that struck a chord in me immediately. Interestingly, when I read the title to the class, there was only a lukewarm reception. Some students still thought it was "corny." As the teacher of the class, I eventually overruled them: the *Swenson Scroll* it was.

My next objective for the class was to give the students a crash course on *news*. What was news, *exactly*? What were its elements? Where did you find it, and how did you report it? Being that it was a beginner's course, I explained to students that news had to be three basic things: *interesting, accurate,* and *important*. We spent a week learning these principles, dissecting newspaper articles, and watching news broadcasts. We talked about sex and violence in news and whether it was the media's job to inform or to entertain. We talked about the difference between *subjectivity* and *objectivity* or, put another way, the difference between opinion and fact. We had lengthy discussions on whether total objectivity in journalism was even *possible*—could news really be "fair and balanced" being that an editor's decision on what news to cover and how to cover it could have serious consequences on the public's perception of the world around them?

After several weeks of introductory work, we got down to the business of writing the school newspaper. It was decided that the paper would be issued twice a semester, so its contents would have to focus on *soft* news—feature stories on current school events, profiles of students or staff, and coverage of Swenson sports teams.

The first step in producing the paper was gathering news. To do this, I had my students research the usual places for stories: I had them check bulletin boards in the counselor's office for scholarships and awards; I had them interview and question coaches and athletes on Swenson's sports teams; I had them gather information on extracurricular clubs and activities; I even had them talk to teachers in the various technology classes about projects and internships.

Students worked on stories together in pairs. Once they were assigned a story, they had to figure out the story's *angle*. This meant deciding on *how* they were going to report the story and *what* they were going to focus on. Basically, this meant showing the students how to go from *general* to *specific*. For example, a story on Swenson's basketball team could have 10 different angles. It could be a profile on the coach, a profile on a player, a summary of a single game or an overview of the entire season. It could be a preview of a play-off game or post-game recap. The choices were many.

I'd make the students write out the angle of their story in one single sentence. If they really *knew* their story and how they wanted to write it, they could effectively capture the idea in one sentence. For example, students covering the boys' basketball team might write, "Our story will summarize the results of Swenson's first regular season game against Martin Luther King High School."

At this stage, I had them focus on how to conduct an interview. I explained to them that when conducting an interview, they should refrain from asking "yes" or "no" questions. I also told them that their questions must always include the five Ws and the H. If a student came back from an interview and they didn't have the who, what, where, when, why, and how of the story, I made them go back and redo it. At the same time, if they returned to class with incomplete facts—if they were missing any dates, times, names, or correct spellings—they would have to return to their source and correct their mistakes.

This process usually took two full weeks, sometimes longer. Once the story's angle was established and the information was gathered, it was time to start *writing* the article. This was a whole process in and of itself. To make things easy, I taught my students about the *inverted pyramid*, the classic template newspapers around the globe had been using to write news stories since the beginning of time. I drew an inverted pyramid on the board, which was an upside-down triangle.

"When you're writing a news story, the most important information comes *first*," I explained to the class. "Right up front in the opening paragraph." I pointed to the inverted pyramid on the board. "You see how the wide part of the triangle is first? Well, this represents the *meat*, the most important facts. As you go down things get thinner, which means the least important facts go last. Why do you think journalists write their stories like this? Lawrence?"

"To get the reader's attention?"

"Right," I said. "To pull the reader in. But news writers also do this to help readers follow the story, to help make it *clear*. And believe it or not, they also do this because of attention spans. Many people are busy, and when they read the newspaper, they only scan the first few paragraphs of a story. When a story gets continued on another page, some people don't bother to keep reading. So in order to give the public the most important information in a story, news writers use the inverted pyramid—they put all the important facts right in the beginning."

Once the students began writing their stories, it usually took the entire 96-minute class period to finish. Most students needed to rewrite their articles at least once before they produced anything worth publishing. It took some students even longer to get it right.

Lawrence, the most enthused student in the class, often rewrote his articles several times before he perfected what he was trying to say. At one point during the semester, Lawrence had come to me with a story he'd written about Swenson's teen pregnancy program. Excited, he showed me his article so I could approve it and put it in the current issue of the *Scroll*.

I read his article with a poker face, but Lawrence saw through it; he knew there was a problem.

"What's wrong with it?" he asked.

"It's too wordy," I told him. "You have this big long introduction, but you don't say much. This is a good start, but where are the facts? Where are the five Ws?"

Lawrence reread his opening paragraph. Then he explained to me that he was trying to grab the reader by telling a mini-story in the opening. I told him that it was good effort and a good idea, but that it wasn't working. His personal anecdote was just confusing things and delaying the real facts of the story.

"Should I rewrite it?" he asked.

"Yes," I told him. "Get right to the facts. Remember, the most important information comes first."

Lawrence nodded, took his paper, and went back to work.

The next day, at the end of class, Lawrence came back up to my desk with his rewritten article and asked me to give it another look. I did. However, it was still too wordy, and I told him so.

"Bullets," I said to him. "You have to write in bullets."

"What's that?"

"It means your sentences need to be short and powerful. Bang! Right to the point. One after the other: bang, bang, bang. Like bullets. What's with all these words, Lawrence? I've read your writing before, and I know you can write much tighter than this. You're thinking too much. You're trying to sound too sophisticated, and you're not saying what you mean. Just say what you mean, real simple. Just *say* it. Don't worry about how it sounds. If you do that, your style will come naturally, so will your voice. Does this make sense?"

Lawrence stood thinking for a minute.

"Bullets," I told him. "Go back and rewrite it. Keep it tight, and get to the facts. Okay?"

"Okay."

The next day Lawrence came back with his article after a third rewrite. I took it from him and read it, quite pleased by his progress.

"Bullets?" he asked me.

"Bullets," I told him. "Congratulations, Lawrence. You made it into the school paper. Nice job, buddy."

"Thanks!"

A week later, when the paper was published, Lawrence was all smiles. So were the 16 other students whose articles had made it into the *Swenson Scroll*. That April, during Swenson's spring parent-teacher conferences, Lawrence's mother came by my classroom to meet me and discuss Lawrence's progress.

"Lawrence really enjoys your class," she told me, proud of her son. "He really respects you as a teacher, too. He talks about your class all the time."

"Thanks," I said. "That's good to hear. Lawrence is a great kid. Excellent student. He always puts in one-hundred-and-ten percent."

Lawrence's mother smiled. "He was just so proud of his article in the school newspaper, let me tell you. He carried it around with him for a week. Showed everybody in the entire family. It's now hanging up on the refrigerator for all to see."

"That's really great to hear," I said. "Good for Lawrence."

I shook hands with Lawrence's mother, and she left. Lawrence would go on to publish two more articles in the paper and finish the class with a 95 average.

The following year, when Lawrence was a senior, I kept up my relationship with him, occasionally seeing him around school and chatting with him in the halls. He looked different his senior year, however. He was thinner by at least 15 pounds. He was also wearing a new hairstyle, keeping his head completely bald. Later, of course, I'd learn that it wasn't a new hairstyle at all, but the aftereffects of chemotherapy. Lawrence had brain cancer and was slowly losing his health. He would fight the good fight and make it to graduation, but shortly after commencement, he passed away.

It happened during the summer, so I didn't find out until the new school year. It was a tough summer for Swenson students. Two other students had died, one in a traffic accident and another by committing suicide. But Lawrence was the hardest to take. I'll never forget his articles in the school newspaper or his passion for writing and his enthusiasm for my class.

SHOWING BY DOING

As students continued to write stories for the *Swenson Scroll*, I was writing articles of my own. In September of 2004, I brought to class an article I had published in the *Philadelphia City Paper* headlined "Philly's Own Al Capone" and an *Inquirer* commentary I had written called "Teacher Pact Bad for Teachers." Both articles, published during teacher contract negotiations between the Philadelphia Federation of Teachers and the School Reform Commission in August and September of 2004, criticize Philadelphia School District CEO Paul Vallas for trying to strip city school teachers of their seniority.

"Teachers work their entire careers to earn the seniority to teach in the best schools," I state in the *Inquirer* piece. "It's madness to think that senior teachers would not harbor bitterness or resentment—both of which could greatly affect their performance in the classroom—over being relegated to a poorly performing school."[1]

In the *City Paper*, I make a similar argument.[2] After we read these articles together as a class, I had the students do the following: identify the thesis and main idea, analyze the supporting arguments, and give their opinions in approximately 100 words.

"Let's look at the article in the *City Paper* first," I said to the class. "What is the thesis? Richard?"

"It's about seniority and the new teachers' contract," Richard said.

"Right, that's the *topic*. That's the subject of the article. But remember, a thesis also has a *viewpoint*. What is the article *saying* about seniority? Leshonda?"

"It's saying that the district shouldn't take away a teacher's seniority, that teachers work their whole careers to work in the best schools and that they shouldn't be forced to go to the worst schools."

I nodded. "Yes, well put. That's the opinion of the article, which happens to be my opinion, because I wrote it. But obviously, you don't have to agree with what I'm saying. Many people don't. There are a number of community groups and education advocates who feel the best teachers should be working in the schools where they are needed most. Unfortunately, these schools sometimes face many challenges and have difficult working conditions, and many teachers don't want to go there. What do you guys think? Should teachers have seniority? Should teachers with the most time and experience be able to select the schools they want to work in? Amanda?"

"Most definitely," she said. "That's only fair. In business and other fields, if you work hard and are successful, you get promoted. You get bonuses and a corner office. Why should teachers be treated any differently? Why should they be forced to work in a school that is violent in the middle of the hood somewhere?"

"Okay," I said, "that's an interesting perspective. Does anyone else have an opinion on the matter? Khalif?"

Khalif waved his hand. "Man, that's prejudiced. You can't say that. Not all schools in the hood are bad. Not all schools in the hood are violent and all that. What? You think kids down in North Philly are all crack babies? That ain't right. That's messed up to say that."

"Good point," I said. "People shouldn't stereotype. Not all schools in the hood are bad. But what about seniority? Should senior teachers with the most experience be able to be transferred to schools where they are needed most?"

"*Yeah*, they should," Khalif said. "They most definitely should. How are poor kids gonna learn? How are they gonna get an education? Good teachers need to go into the bad schools so kids can finally start to learn."

"Thanks, Khalif," I said. "That's definitely a valid argument. There are many people out there who feel the way you do. Hopefully a compromise will be made soon. The rights of the teachers need to be respected, and so do the rights of the children trying to learn." I paused for a moment, looking at the clock. "Unfortunately, we have to move on. We have a few more things to cover in class today. Now if you would, let's get out our journalism textbooks and open to page eighty-five. I want to look at something called 'attribution,' which is a big word that simply means giving someone credit for a quote or source of information. Stacy, would you begin reading that first paragraph please . . ."

The students got out their books and we continued the lesson.

NOTES

1. Christopher Paslay, "Teacher Pact Bad for Teachers," *Philadelphia Inquirer*, August 12, 2004.
2. Christopher Paslay, "Philly's Own Al Capone," *Philadelphia City Paper*, September 9-16, 2004.

FOURTEEN
Politics

It's no secret politics affect education. As Rita Kramer, distinguished author and social critic writes in *Ed School Follies: The Miseducation of America's Teachers*:

> Those who are trained in the vocations of law and medicine profess to know more than their clients about their fields and their clients' needs; they work independently and not under bureaucratic control; and they possess a fixed body of specific knowledge. In contrast, teachers are directed in their daily work by political bodies outside their field, and their training institutions have no agreed-on disciplinary content.[1]

In other words, politicians outside the field of education shape the landscape of America's public schools. Unfortunately, too often a legislator's policies on education are influenced not by sound ideas but by outside agendas. Money has a way of influencing school reform, as do jobs and contracts.

An example of the blurred boundaries between profits and education was the debacle involving Edison Schools Inc., a private education management organization, and the Philadelphia School District. In 2002, when Act 46 required the state of Pennsylvania to take over Philadelphia schools because of failing test scores, Governor Mark Schweiker, a Republican, proposed turning the entire district over to Edison, a deal that could have given the for-profit consultant hundreds of millions of dollars. After resistance by Philadelphia Mayor John Street and community groups, Schweiker backed a plan to give a six-year, $101 million contract to Edison Schools, which would have given the private manager control of 45 of the city's neediest schools.[2]

In August of 2002, when a total of 70 of Philadelphia's worst performing schools were targeted for takeover or restructuring, 45 were doled out to outside managers. Edison was eventually given control of only 20 schools and paid $11.8 million for the 2002–2003 school year.³ The remaining 25 were to be turned into charters or reconstituted and run by the district. To ensure the improvement of these schools, the state approved $83 million in funds to be given to the district. As it turned out, however, state secretary of education Charles B. Zogby had lobbied that $55 million of it be spent on the outside managers. "That condition prompted cries of cronyism, since Edison has long-standing ties to the Republican Pennsylvania governor's office," writes Catherine Gewertz in a 2002 *Education Week* article.⁴

Money isn't always the root of the problem. Politicians also manipulate educational policy to win votes, shape public perception, and advance party agendas. Worse still, they sometimes operate out of sheer ignorance and base their decisions on impartial information or even misinformation.

An example of this was Pennsylvania state senator Jeffrey E. Piccola's Education Empowerment Act. Proposed in 2010, the bill fought to reform public education in Pennsylvania by giving the state and individual districts more power to hand failing schools over to private managers or turn them into charters. "Piccola said much of his proposal builds on academic gains in Philadelphia during the last decade, which he attributed to opening dozens of charters and turning schools over to education-management organizations," writes Dan Hardy of the *Philadelphia Inquirer*.⁵

Although Piccola may have had the best interest of children in mind, he was clearly misinformed. Philadelphia schools run by private managers in the first decade of the 21st century did *not* show any improvement. In fact, scores *lagged behind*. A report prepared by the Accountability Review Council for the Philadelphia School Reform Commission in February of 2007 shows that from 2002 to 2006, PSSA (Pennsylvania System of School Assessment) scores went up 23 percent in math and 14.5 percent in reading in district-managed schools, while schools run by education management organizations only had gains of 19.6 in math and 11.9 in reading.⁶ In other words, traditional public schools outperformed private managers across the board. Somehow Piccola missed or ignored this fact completely.

New Jersey governor Chris Christi did much of the same in September of 2010 when he proposed tying teacher pay to student achievement.⁷ Curiously, one week before he announced this proposal, the results of a major study on teacher performance pay were released with the following conclusion: *performance pay doesn't work*. The study involved almost 300 middle school math teachers in Nashville, Tennessee.⁸

Did Christi miss this major study or simply ignore it? Was Christi genuinely interested in student achievement, or was his proposal to tie teacher pay to student performance a political move to embrace the popular theme of "accountability" to win votes? If the study was ignored, it further highlighted the blurry boundary between politics and education.

REPUBLICAN VERSUS DEMOCRAT

Over the last half century, both Republicans and Democrats have had their own separate vision for "fixing" America's public schools. Although some reforms have been embraced by both parties, a pattern has emerged between the two. Generally speaking, Republicans have lobbied for school choice in an effort to create competition and improve the quality of public schools. This "choice" has relied heavily on schools run by education management organizations (EMOs), school vouchers, and the expansion of charter schools.

These reforms have gotten mixed results. The evidence seems solid that EMOs are struggling to increase student achievement and are not worth the money. A 2006 story in *Education Week* sums up their effectiveness this way:

> Researchers at the American Institutes for Research screened 940 studies on seven different educational management organizations to look for proof of whether the programs produce gains in student achievement. Only nine studies met the group's strict definition for scientific quality and all of them focused on Edison Schools, a New York City-based for-profit company that operates 157 schools around the country. But even that evidence was not enough to warrant Edison an effectiveness rating any stronger than "moderate" by the research group's standards. No providers earned AIR's top two ratings: "moderately strong" and "very strong."[9]

School vouchers, the policy of giving parents public funds to send their children to private schools, have had some success in raising the achievement of low-income minority students. However, studies on the impact of school vouchers vary as do their interpretations.[10]

Charter schools, like vouchers, have also had some success in raising achievement. Of course, they are not without their critics. Some claim charters skim the "cream" from the traditional schools, leaving the poor and underprivileged behind. Supporters of charters will deny that this is the case. They will explain that technically, charters cannot hand-select their clientele. They will explain that by law, charters must give all students a fair shot at gaining admissions, which is why charters hold lotteries to decide which students will be given admittance.

Although this is technically true, successful charters still manage to draw the most functional students because of two factors: (1) the charter school admissions process is much more stringent than that of traditional schools, requiring parents to serve as an advocate for their child and get actively involved in their schooling; and (2) charter schools have the ability to remove problem students with discipline or academic issues more readily than neighborhood schools.

Whether it comes to EMOs, school vouchers, or charter schools, one thing has become clear: Republicans have basically given up on traditional urban education. It's been dominated by Democrats for so long, by liberal mayors, by liberal superintendents, by liberal school boards, by liberal parents. Why should Republicans bother? It's better for them to turn their backs on the whole mess. It's easier to enact laws that will, in effect, extract the children of their constituency from the problem than try to roll up their sleeves and fight the good fight.

This is where the Democrats step in. They have built their reforms around the mantra of *educational equity*. Competition and choice aren't always the answer, especially when the educational playing field is, in many cases, lopsided, as well as the home environment, the availability of jobs and resources, the condition of neighborhood schools and classrooms, and the quality of neighborhood teachers and administrators.

Although Democrats, like many Republicans, have been willing to experiment with charter schools, some haven't been as willing to pump money into unproven for-profit EMOs. In late 2001, when Pennsylvania governor Mark Schweiker lobbied to have Edison Schools run the Philadelphia School District's central administration, Philadelphia mayor John Street, a Democrat, objected, and community protests soon erupted. Activists blocked streets and carried signs that read, "Our Children Are Not for Sale."[11]

Not that the Democrats haven't been willing to spend money on educating the urban underprivileged. The Philadelphia School District, a school system in a city that hasn't had a Republican mayor in over 50 years, had a budget of $3.043 billion for the 2009–2010 fiscal year. This was a quarter-billion dollar increase over its 2008–2009 budget of $2.794 billion.[12] The jump in funds was primarily the result of state and federal stimulus money, provided by both a Democrat governor (Ed Rendell), and a Democrat president (Barack Obama).

Democrats have been using large amounts of money to try to close achievement gaps for some time. In 1965, President Lyndon B. Johnson, a Democrat, passed the Elementary and Secondary Education Act. The most recognizable section of the act was Title I. Title I allocates special funds to help improve the schools and facilities attended by children from low-income families. Over the years, billions have been spent on the program with questionable results. "Despite being conducted by people who wished the program well, no evaluation of Title I from the 1970s onward has found credible evidence of a significant positive impact on student achievement," writes noted scholar and social scientist Charles Murray in 2008.[13]

Liberals have also been big on diversity and racial balancing to try to bring about educational equity. The school desegregation movement initiated in the South in the 1950s is a well-known example. Integration, however, did not end there. The push to diversify student bodies in schools across America has been steady. The use of affirmative action and special recruiting programs to hire K–12 minority teachers has also been used. In June of 2009, the Philadelphia School Reform Commission voted to spend $250,000 to hire a Florida consulting firm to help hire 50 black teachers to work in the Philadelphia city schools for the 2009–10 school year.[14] In the end, the district fell terribly short of its goal.

Interestingly, as of 2010, gaps in graduation rates between urban and suburban public schools remained large. As for closing the achievement gap between black and white children who attend K–12 public schools, there has only been "modest" progress.[15]

When it comes to significantly raising the achievement of all children, neither the Republicans nor the Democrats seem to have the magic answer.

CONCRETE VERSUS ABSTRACT

A 2008 study published in the *Journal of Political Psychology* revealed an interesting finding about the bedrooms and workplaces of conservatives and liberals: conservative's spaces tended to be orderly whereas liberal's tended to be cluttered.[16] Dana Carney, who coauthored the study, explains that a conservative's cognitive inclination toward order and a liberal's toward ambiguity and intellectualism "drive the way one leads one's life and displays one's life in their living and work spaces."[17]

The fact that conservatives tend to be more orderly and concrete and that liberals tend to prefer ambiguity and intellectualism over rigid structure has a curious way of manifesting itself in the world of public education. When it comes to urban education, where Democrats have had majority rule, traditional, high-structured teaching methods have been marginalized. Direct instruction—drills, rote memorization, and formulaic exercises once used to build rudimentary skills and fundamental mechanics—has been shunned as outdated and ineffectual.

The whole-language movement is one example. It downplayed phonics and the decoding of words in favor of using "high quality" literature to teach reading. The same situation evolved with "new math." Progressive reformers devalued the mastery of teacher-taught math fundamentals in favor of using student-centered creativity and reasoning to find solutions to problems.

Not surprisingly, project-based group instruction has been pushed with great fervor. Teacher-centered lessons, where instruction is highly structured and organized, has been replaced by more student-centered learning activities. In the 21st century, teachers are groomed to be a "guide on the side" rather than the "sage on the stage." Learning should involve physical activity—kids moving and talking with moderate volumes of educational noise. In the 21st century, a quiet classroom is a *boring* classroom, and a boring classroom couldn't possibly involve any real learning.

The same holds true with academic tracking. Tracking is clean and organized and allows teachers to deal with one ability level at a time. There isn't as great a need for differentiated instruction because student skill sets are more uniform. Heterogeneously grouped classes, conversely, are messier and harder to both teach and manage. Dealing with diverse groups of students on varying ability levels all at the same time— including English language learners and mainstreamed special education students—can, at times, cause instruction to become a generic melting pot of ideas and skills.

This generic quality, of course, isn't inherently bad. In fact, it helps close the distribution of achievement so the struggling students don't fall too far behind and the high achievers don't pull too far ahead. While the average achievement of students hasn't changed significantly in the past 50 years, "the acquired verbal skills of gifted American students have declined dramatically, as illustrated by the trends in the SAT-Verbal test," writes Charles Murray. "This decline cannot be blamed on changes in the SAT pool. It's based on all seventeen-year-olds. Some sort of failure to educate the gifted is to blame."[18] This, in effect, satisfies the goal of most progressives, which is educational equity and social justice. Put another way, it's fairness for the sake of being fair.

Republicans, on the other hand, like competition. And the best way to compete is to clearly define the rules and eliminate any ambiguity or gray areas. When it comes to instruction, the *teacher* runs the show, not the students. Rules are set and routines are established. Everything is organized and measureable so there can be no foolery or slacking off. Students either know the answer or they don't, perform on the test or don't, and there is no slipping through the cracks; there is no hiding behind a buddy or fellow group member.

Not surprisingly, many suburban and higher socioeconomic school districts still track their students. Not surprisingly, many of the families whose children attend these schools are conservative. And when these neat, clean, tracked schools with exemplary organization start to get a little less organized—a little less uniform and a little more integrated and diverse—then these conservative families demand the freedom guaranteed by our Constitution and lobby for free market competition—or put another way, *charter schools*; if you can't beat 'em, just run away from 'em.

While conservatives are fighting for neatness and organization in their schools and communities, liberals are, as previously noted, calling for social justice. In a certain sense, social justice, which is maddeningly ambiguous in and of itself, can be viewed as the antithesis of neatness and organization, of establishment, of order and control. Social justice is basically a monkey wrench in the system of the ruling class. What kind of monkey wrench? Doesn't matter. Any monkey wrench will do. Anything that eliminates economic boundaries, social privileges, and educational and class distinctions is a positive. Structure is bad. Ambiguity is good.

In terms of educational strategies, one example of this is the use of the classic five-paragraph essay to teach writing. Over the years, I've run into a number of liberal college professors who have treated the five-paragraph essay like the plague. Each time the topic is brought up, I get the same argument: *writing, real, meaningful writing, is a non-linear process*. To force students into a suffocating set-structure is to stifle their creativity. On one hand, I agree. I've written enough words in my life to know my best stuff comes when I don't try to write it from beginning to end. My best work comes when I just jump to it, dive right in, without worrying about intros or salutations. Ray Bradbury once wrote about the art of writing, "In quickness is truth. The faster you blurt, the more swiftly you write, the more honest you are. In delay comes the effort for a style, instead of leaping upon truth which is the *only* style worth deadfalling or tiger-trapping."[19]

I agree with Bradbury wholeheartedly. To hesitate, to squeeze yourself into a structure, can impede your writing. However, this is at the higher levels of the craft. This is the case only after you have enough familiarity with the written word that composing introductions, bodies, and conclusions is like chewing gum, that incorporating evidence into an argument is like sneezing. If you can't grasp the concept of a thesis, if you stumble over opening paragraphs, over writing a closing, Bradbury's observations won't do you much good.

I often explain this fact to my liberal counterparts, only to have them scoff at me. *The five-paragraph essay is a recipe for mush*, they insist. I beg to differ. Students need to crawl before they can walk. And in my experience, many come into my classroom barely able to get on their hands and knees. What they need is a *structure*, a template, a step-by-step diagram. They need to see it, and they need to hold it in their hands. Otherwise, their heads are left spinning.

This reality applies to more than just writing. It applies to almost everything in the urban classroom, including math, science, social studies, foreign language, study skills, self discipline, anger management, and so forth. Students with chaotic lives, especially those whose home lives lack guidance, crave structure. If you put up a fence in the backyard, a kid doesn't have to think about the boundaries anymore, he can run free within the limits. Without a fence, a kid might forget himself and get hurt, wander off and get lost, fall down a well, get hit by a car. Unfortunately, trends in urban education have eliminated a fair amount of fences when it comes to instruction and pedagogy.

With conservatives turning their backs on the messiness of urban education and pushing for "choice" outside neighborhood schools, a progressive liberal vacuum has been created in the inner city; although, Democrats also support charters, enough have stood in support of traditional schools to have claimed the territory by default. This liberal dominance of education has been taking place for some time. As Rita Kramer writes in *Ed School Follies*:

> The "new left" social scientists who came on the scene in the late 1960s began to reinterpret American history and sociology from a predominantly Marxist point of view, and nowhere were the revisionists more radical than in the field of schooling. The books by Kozol, Goodman, Illich, and others became best sellers and their ideas about the relationship between school and society, teacher and pupil, permeated the ed. school world, both in terms of what was taught and how research was designed, carried out, and interpreted.[20]

This liberal influence has contributed to a brand of socialistic educational policy that too frequently frowns upon concreteness and competition. Pedagogy that waters down learning, disguised as instruction that increases rigor, has been taking root in large urban districts. Democrats should be praised for not turning their backs on urban education and rallying for educational equity, but they can't do it alone. Conservatives must rejoin the fight to bring on competition and balance policy. And they must do it *inside* the neighborhood schools, not outside in a charter or private school.

ABILITY LEVEL AND EDUCATIONAL ROMANTICISM

The fight for educational equity is a battle that must be won. All students, regardless of race or socioeconomic status, must receive a quality education. Determining whether or not students have received one, however, is the tricky part. Educational equity means equal opportunity, but it goes beyond that. It also implies equal *achievement*. In other words, many people (especially politicians and those looking to exploit education for personal gains) reason that if all students aren't scoring equally on standardized achievement tests, then all of these children mustn't be receiving equal educations.

This isn't necessarily true. There's no disputing that America's public school system has much room to improve. There's also no disputing that too many children have been shortchanged when it comes to receiving a quality education. However, even if all children *had* been given equal instruction across the board, even if they *had* been given the best teachers and the best schools and the best resources, not all children would score equally on standardized tests.

Let's suppose we had the kind of education system politicians promised—one with equal resources and teachers and schools. If all children in this system were to take an achievement test that measured whether or not they were on grade level in a specific subject and if "grade level" was defined as the tasks that someone of average academic ability could be taught to do, then approximately *half* the children would score below grade level. That's nothing more than the law of averages.

During the 2009–2010 school year, the Philadelphia School District reached a new milestone: the majority of its students were on grade level in reading and math, which meant they had scored either proficient or advanced on the annual PSSA test. When I say *majority*, I mean 57 percent were on grade level in math, and 51 percent were on grade level in reading.[21] The curious thing about these numbers is that they fall right around the halfway point mentioned previously. Average means the *middle*—half are above, half are below. The concept is similar to the median price of a home in a particular neighborhood. No matter the neighborhood, or the average value of the houses, *half* the homes are going to be below the median price when dealing with large numbers of houses. Imagine if a real estate agent insisted that *all* homes in a neighborhood be the median price? This would only be possible when all homes became the *exact* same price.

Student ability levels are real, and they vary. Not many people want to accept this, especially politicians who want your vote or education management organizations who want your business or community organizations who want your support. To quote Charles Murray, "We are phobic about saying out loud that children differ in their ability to learn the things that schools teach. Not only do we hate to say it, we get angry with people who do. We insist that the emperor *is* wearing clothes, beautiful clothes, and that those who say otherwise are bad people. Call it educational romanticism."[22]

All kids can learn but in different degrees. Educators in America must continue to set high expectations and challenge all students, but they mustn't do so wearing rose-colored glasses. All children have their strengths and weaknesses. Public schools must work hard to see that all children reach their potential, but this potential should not be limited to several core academic subjects. Learning is much broader than this. As Chris Myers Asch, a history teacher at the University of the District of Columbia, writes in *American Educator* in 2010:

> We have so effectively pushed the notion that "success equals college" that other options, such as vocational education, seem horribly limiting and even discriminatory. But college prep has become a one-size-fits-all approach to secondary education, and some students simply do not fit.... College is not always the best choice for students whose interests and skills lend themselves to trades rather than a college degree.[23]

In other words, children who score below average in English and math might be excellent musicians, athletes, carpenters, or electricians. They might be wizards in the culinary arts. They might be able to repair a smashed fender or fix a fuel-injector blindfolded and standing on one leg. Schools must understand this reality and work hard to help all students of differing skills and ability levels achieve all of their dreams.

NOTES

1. Rita Kramer, *Ed School Follies: The Miseducation of America's Teachers* (Lincoln, NE: iUniverse, 2000), 8.
2. Catherine Gewertz, "Phila. Lines Up Outside Groups to Run Schools," *Education Week*, August 7, 2002, 1, 18–19.
3. Gewertz, "Phila. Lines Up," 1, 18–19.
4. Gewertz, "Phila. Lines Up," 1, 18–19.
5. Dan Hardy, "Pa. Bill Would Expand Overhaul of Schools," *Philadelphia Inquirer*, February 8, 2010.
6. Accountability Review Council, *Report to the School Reform Commission: The Status of 2005–2006 Academic Performance in the School District of Philadelphia* (Philadelphia, PA: Philadelphia School District, February, 2007), 5–6, http://webgui.phila.k12.pa.us/uploads/VI/MW/VIMW9vzAYe8S_4mzIeditQ/ARC-Report-_Feb-7-07.pdf (accessed August 8, 2010).
7. Cynthia Henry, "Christie Proposes Changes in How Teachers Are Paid, Promoted," *Philadelphia Inquirer*, September 29, 2010.
8. Stephen Sawchuk, "Merit Pay Found to Have Little Effect on Achievement," *Education Week*, September 21, 2010, www.edweek.org/ew/articles/2010/09/21/05pay_ep.h30.html?qs=performance+pay.
9. Debra Viadero, "Research Group Rates Effectiveness of Educational Management Organizations," *Education Week*, April 24, 2006, www.edweek.org/ew/articles/2006/04/24/33air_web.h25.html?qs=Studies+on+EMOs.
10. Martin Carnoy, *School Vouchers: Examining the Evidence* (Washington, DC: Economic Policy Institute, 2001), 2–3.
11. Catherine Gewertz, "Phila. Takeover Deadline Marked by Protests," *Education Week*, December 5, 2001, 5.
12. Michael J. Masch, *School District of Philadelphia: Revised Budget Presentation to the School Reform Commission, Fiscal Year 2009–10* (Philadelphia: Philadelphia School District, December 6, 2009), 5, http://webgui.phila.k12.pa.us/uploads/3P/t2/3Pt2U9VMxhTISZ_cqxyUNQ/09-11-18-SDP-FY10-Rvsd-Bgt-SRC-PPT.pdf (accessed August 8, 2010).
13. Charles Murray, *Real Education: Four Simple Truths for Bringing America's Schools Back to Reality* (New York: Three Rivers, 2008), 60.
14. "Newsflash July 2009: At the SRC . . ." *Philadelphia Public School Notebook*, July, 2009, www.thenotebook.org/july-2009/091513/src .
15. Sean Cavanagh, "Black-White Achievement," *Education Week*, August 12, 2009, 5.
16. Dana R. Carney, John T. Jost, Samuel D. Gosling, and Jeff Potter, "The Secret Lives of Liberals and Conservatives: Personality Profiles, Interaction Styles, and the Things They Leave Behind," *Political Psychology* 29, no. 6 (2008): 832.
17. Jordan Lite, "Political Science: What Being Neat or Messy Says about Political Leanings," *Scientific American*, October 13, 2008, www.scientificamerican.com/article.cfm?id=organization-and-political-leanings.
18. Murray, *Real Education*, 114.
19. Ray Bradbury, *Zen in the Art of Writing* (New York: Bantam Books, 1992), 13.

20. Kramer, *Ed School Follies*, 8.
21. Kristen A. Graham, "A Test-Score Milestone for Phila. Schools," *Philadelphia Inquirer*, June 17, 2010.
22. Murray, *Real Education*, 11.
23. Chris Myers Asch, *American Educator*, Fall 2010, 9.

FIFTEEN
Later Years

In 2007, when I began teaching creative writing, I had my students compose a screenplay for a short film. I used Syd Field's book *Screenplay: The Foundations of Screenwriting* as a basis for the unit. The first thing I covered in class was that a screenplay was different from a play and different from a fiction story. I explained that a screenplay was a *script*—it told the director what to shoot and the actors what to say. I also told them that one page of script usually equaled one minute of screen time, regardless if the page was all dialogue, all description, or a combination of the two.

"If a movie is two hours long," I asked the class that first week, "how many pages will its script be? Harold?"

"Uhm . . . one-hundred-and-twenty pages?"

"Bingo."

I went over the structure of a screenplay. I showed them that just like any story, a screenplay has a beginning, a middle, and an end. I also told them about what Syd Field called "plot points," the events in the script that spin the action from the beginning to the middle and the middle to the end.

Once all my students grasped the structure of a screenplay, I introduced the project for the quarter: to write a script for a 30-minute short film. The kids quickly did the math and realized this meant they would have to write a *30-page screenplay*. Interestingly, no one complained. In fact, I got the opposite reaction from the class: students got excited about it.

The first step of the project, I explained to them, was to brainstorm for movie ideas.

"Think about what kind of movies you like to watch," I told them. "Do you like horror? Comedy? Romance? Science fiction? Action? Drama? What? Once you have an idea what genre you want to write about, then you need to ask yourself the next question: who is going to be the main character? This is perhaps the most important part of your story — your *protagonist*. Remember, what is a story? Who can tell me? Anybody? Regine?"

"A story has a beginning, middle, and end," Regine told me.

"Okay, that's true, they are the *parts* of a story. But that's not what a story *is*. Who can tell me what a story *is*? What *is* story?"

No one raised their hands.

"Story is what happens to a person we've been led to care about. *That's* story. In other words, a good story will involve a main character that hooks us in. If we're not invested in the character, if we don't give a crap about whether she lives or dies, succeeds or fails, then there's no real story there. Does this make any sense?"

The kids nodded and said that it did.

We worked on generating plot outlines and creating characters for two weeks. It wasn't until the third week of class that the students actually starting *writing* their screenplays. This was clearly the most difficult part of the process because it involved teaching the kids how to write in script format. Script format, at first glance, seemed overwhelming to the students; it seemed overwhelming to me the first time I saw it 15 years earlier. However, after you broke it down into four or five elements, it really wasn't that complicated.

For two whole days, we read and analyzed actual scripts, sometimes watching clips from films to see how the action translated onto the screen. It was then that students learned about FADE IN and FADE OUT, about something called a "slug line," about how to center dialogue under a character's name. They learned that EXT stood for "exterior," which meant that a particular scene would take place *outside*. Likewise, they learned that INT stood for "interior," which meant that the scene would take place *inside*.

The first eight pages of each student's screenplay were due the second week of October. The students brought their scripts to class, typed in proper format, and proceeded to peer-edit them with a partner. After they were proofed by their classmates, they submitted them to me, and I further identified mistakes and gave suggestions for improvement. A month later, the next 15 pages were due. These portions were also edited accordingly. Finally, the second week of December, the entire 30-page script was due.

Amazingly, I received a script from every student except two. Nearly all of the screenplays I received were neatly typed and almost 30 pages long. I was quite stunned by this, being that in years past I couldn't even get my students to produce *ten* pages of script. But 30 pages I got, complete with plot points and clean resolutions and well-developed characters.

I read the screenplays over Christmas break, impressed with the effort put forth. The scripts were creative and entertaining. One was a comedy about a drug dealer who sold marijuana that gave people x-ray vision. Another was a thriller about a man who stalked an ex-girlfriend because he was obsessed with the smell of her shampoo. It was titled "Herbal Essence," and in the end, the guy cuts off all of his former lover's hair. There were also plenty of steamy romances penned by the ladies in the class. Most involved lots of cheating, lots of name-calling, and lots of cops issuing restraining orders.

In the new year, I ended the unit by requiring my students to write a one-page query letter and pitch their movie idea to an actual Hollywood script agency. I purchased the *2007 Guide to Literary Agents* and gave the kids a choice of several agencies to which to write. I paid for the stamps and took their letters to the post office when they were finished writing them. I did this not because I hoped to get a response, but to teach my students the actual process of trying to find an agent. This is why three weeks later, when a boy named Oscar informed me that he'd received a call from one of the Hollywood agencies, I was stunned and completely surprised.

"They liked my movie idea," he told me, all smiles. "I spoke to a woman named Joyce and told her I was still in high school. She told me that she wanted to talk with my creative writing teacher." Oscar handed me a slip of paper. "Here's her number. She wants you to call her."

I congratulated Oscar and took the paper from him. Later that afternoon, I made the call to Joyce, speaking to her at length, explaining my screenplay assignment, going over the lessons I'd been doing with my students.

"That's excellent," she told me. "I'm so glad to hear that public school teachers are helping kids get excited about script writing." She went on to give me some pointers about writing proposals and query letters and told me to keep up the good work. She also informed me that although she liked Oscar's movie idea, she was unfortunately going to have to pass on it; it became clear that the only reason she called was because she was interested in my assignment, not in Oscar's script.

The next day in class, I told Oscar that I had spoken with Joyce about his movie idea and that we both agreed that he had talent. Then, as gently as possible, I broke the news to him that the agency was passing on his idea. Oscar told me that it was cool, that he didn't care, but I could see the disappointment on his face.

"Just keep writing," I told him. "Your day will come."

Later in class, I announced the bittersweet news to my creative writing students: Oscar's movie idea had received some interest from a Hollywood agency, but in the end, they decided not to use it. The students gathered around Oscar's desk and congratulated him and did their best to cheer him up. I went over and shook Oscar's hand and once again told him not to let this roadblock get him down.

That year in class, the students would go on to write several poems, a short story, a picture book, and a mini-autobiography. Although they would produce some interesting work, none of it surpassed the quality and creativity of their 30-page screenplays.

RAISING THE READING BAR

As the 2009–2010 school year began, Dr. Ackerman, along with U.S. education secretary Arne Duncan, continued to push the theme of accountability. The threat of overhauling schools that didn't meet standards in reading and math loomed large over the district. As a response to this threat, principals began stepping up their focus on literacy and math. At the high school level, this meant concentrating interventions on the 11th grade, being that it was the standardized reading and math scores of 11th-grade students that counted for Annual Yearly Progress (AYP) under the federal No Child Left Behind law.

In 2009–2010, I was Swenson's only 11th-grade English teacher, which meant I taught the entire junior class English. Although it was the whole school's responsibility to ensure that all students were proficient in both reading and math, it was no secret that 11th-grade teachers were under an added pressure to produce. To raise scores that year, I decided to go back to the basics of literacy. It was time to *read*, then read some more. And when the reading was done, we would turn to writing.

For many teenagers, reading long passages of text was too abstract and required too much concentration. Besides, in the 21st century, reading was *so yesterday*. If what you had to say couldn't fit on the two-inch screen of a cell phone—if you couldn't send it via a quick text to your buddy—forget about it. It was too much trouble. Plus, most of the reading in the district's 11th-grade English curriculum was too tame for the tastes of many teenagers—it lacked the requisite amount of sex and violence to make it appealing.

Tragically, these were the challenges our school was presented with while trying to raise reading scores in 2010. I pushed on nonetheless. I did what I could do to bring in high interest reading, and once a week, I had students read and dissect a commentary from the *Philadelphia Inquirer*. Some weeks, I used my own articles to keep them interested.

To raise the bar in terms of rigor, I started focusing on rhetorical skills. Students were not only required to know *how* a piece of text was written, but *why* it was written that way. What was the author's purpose? Did he or she achieve that purpose? What was the tone? Why was this tone used? Were the author's arguments appeals to logic or emotion? Why? What evidence was given?

To supplement their reading skills, I did a lot of writing, not creative writing, but formal, structured essays. I had them write a number of persuasive essays on a current event. I had them present these essays in the front of the class, detailing their thesis, arguments, and supporting evidence. Then I'd challenge their arguments, and we'd debate the issue. The sharp students held their own, able to articulate their ideas and expound upon them. The students who were not as strong linguistically sometimes stammered and faded, but I forced them to the edge of their comfort zones, challenging them to improve nonetheless.

Once in a while, a student refused to present his or her essay in front of the class altogether. This happened one time with a young lady named Madeline, who had written an essay about same-sex marriage. Although she refused to present, I kept at her, coaxing her to come to the front of the room and just give it a shot.

"Come on," I said to her. "If you refuse to present, you're going to fail the paper."

She shook her head. "I don't care. I'll take a zero."

I walked over to her desk. "You know, it's okay if you're nervous. *Everybody's* nervous presenting in front of the class. Do you know what the number one fear in America is?"

She shook her head and said that she didn't.

"Public speaking," I told her. "Nobody likes doing it. But it's no big deal. Just come on up and give it a shot. It's not as bad as you think."

"I can't do it," she insisted.

"I'll tell you what," I said. "Just start by standing up, that's it. You don't even have to say anything. Just get up and stand here in front of the room, and I'll give you partial credit."

"Seriously?"

"Yep. Just come up here and stand in front of the room."

Madeline got up and stood at the front of the class.

I smiled. "Great job. Was that so hard?"

She nodded nervously. "No."

"Good. Now just tell us your topic. What did you write about?"

"Same-sex marriage."

"Okay, good. Are you for it or against it?"

"For it."

"Why are you for it?"

"Because all people deserve equal rights, even gays and lesbians."

"Awesome. You're doing great. Why else are you for same-sex marriage?"

Something in Madeline loosened. "Gays and lesbians should be able to get married so they can share health insurance," she said and proceeded to go into her other arguments, quoting the U.S. Constitution and even using her own sexuality as an example. The class listened attentively, drawn in by her sincerity and passion, and when she finished, the room broke out in loud applause.

"Great job," I told her. "See, I knew you could do it."

"Thanks, Mr. Paslay," she said, her hands shaking slightly from all her emotion. Smiling, she sat down.

For the rest of the year, we continued reading and analyzing text. We practiced sample PSSA reading prompts and worked on strategies to answer the constructed response questions. We did vocabulary, deconstructed text, and read some more. My focus on literacy, along with the help of the English Department and the entire Swenson faculty and community as a whole, would ultimately pay off. That spring, 46.7 percent of Swenson 11th-graders would score proficient or advanced in reading, beating the previous year's scores by 15 points and giving Swenson's junior class the highest PSSA reading scores in the history of the school.[1] On the writing portion of the PSSA, our juniors would score *70 percent* proficient or advanced, just 10 points under the 2010 state test average of 80 percent.

When I was given the official results, the first thing I did was find my students and congratulate them. I was especially proud of Madeline, who scored advanced in reading and proficient in writing.

"You're quite the expert reader," I told her one day in the hallway.

"Thanks," she said and smiled.

Things had come quite a long way since my first year on the job in 1997.

NOTE

1. "Swenson Arts and Technology, PSSA, Grade 11 Reading," Philadelphia School District, https://webapps.philasd.org/school_profile/view/8090.

SIXTEEN
Pop Culture and Technology

In 1991, a New York City schoolteacher named John Taylor Gatto published a book called *Dumbing Us Down: The Hidden Curriculum of Compulsory Schooling*. The premise of the book is that America's educational system was programming students to conform to the norms of society rather than teaching them how to become freethinkers. The book was a success in part because of the uniqueness of its author. Gatto was a three-time New York City Teacher of the Year as well as a New York state Teacher of the Year. Incredibly, at the height of his career, Gatto quit teaching. He did so famously by announcing his decision on the op-ed page of the *Wall Street Journal* in 1991, explaining that he no longer wanted to hurt kids to make a living.[1]

Gatto's assertion that schools are producing mindless individuals programmed to become cogs in a larger societal wheel is curious because it is the exact opposite of what I've known to be true after a decade and a half of teaching: society isn't the result of our school system; our school system is the result of our society.

America in the 21st century is brimming with technology. Cell phones and the Internet have enabled people to communicate instantaneously with loved ones around the globe. Banking can be done electronically, as can shopping, dating, applying for unemployment, sending out resumes, and all manner of tasks that used to be done in person. GPS systems have rendered road maps obsolete and E-ZPass transponders have nullified the need for drivers to stop to pay tolls.

This advancement in technology has brought an obvious change in culture. The old proverb "Good things come to those who wait" no longer applies in the 21st century. In today's society, Americans don't wait; patience is no longer a virtue. Waiting is a sign of inferiority and even social ineptness, like the man in the Visa Check Card commercial who has the audacity to stop at the register to pay for his purchase with cash, not with the clean swipe of his debit card, disrupting the rhythm of the entire line behind him. In short, America has become an instant-gratification society addicted to technology. And it is this very addiction that is taking a toll on our schools.

LITERACY AND ATTENTION SPANS

America not only continues to push the message that it is inconvenient to have patience and wait for things, but also it shortens our children's attention spans through television and video games. A 2010 study published in the journal *Pediatrics* concludes: "Viewing television and playing video games each are associated with increased subsequent attention problems in childhood. It seems that a similar association among television, video games, and attention problems exists in late adolescence and early adulthood."[2]

This is disturbing news, being that our country is hooked on these forms of entertainment, especially television. According to a 2009 Nielsen report, the average American watched over 151 hours of television a month—the equivalent of about 5 hours a day. More shocking was the fact that the average U.S. household contained more TVs than people.[3]

When it comes to literacy and education in general, attention span is everything. Kids can't learn if they can't concentrate. Although the skills involved with reading comprehension are complex, if children can't focus on a passage long enough to decode and absorb it, there's no way they'll understand what they're reading. Unfortunately, when it comes to literacy, the situation is a catch-22. To be a good reader, you need to practice. To practice, you need an attention span. If you don't have an attention span, practicing reading will be uncomfortable, and the odds are you won't do much of it. And therein lies the problem.

I see this all the time with the high school students I teach. Their biggest complaint is that they don't like reading, that it's uncomfortable. This is obviously nothing new. Back in the 1980s, when I went to school, it was common to hear my fiends complaining about reading. The same held true for my mother and father in the 1960s. However, things have gotten worse in the 21st century. Comfort levels in reading have gotten pathetically low. This is not only the case in American classrooms but also in society as a whole.

During the summer of 2010, I was in a large bookstore shopping for reading material in preparation for a week at the Jersey Shore with my wife. For a change of pace, I decided to buy a few magazines instead of books. Because I'm fascinated by the outdoors, I decided to pick up *Outside* magazine and peruse its pages. As I did so, I began to get frustrated. *Where are the articles?* I wondered. I continued looking through the magazine for several minutes longer, but the problem still remained—there were no articles. I went back to the front of the magazine and started again, flipping through the pages in search of a nice, healthy passage to read.

That's when I realized my mistake: the articles where there, but in most cases, they were short and neatly packaged to run no longer than a page. They were also dressed-up with fancy headlines and glossy pictures and all sorts of other eye-catching embellishments. It was the embellishments that threw me; I thought they were advertisements. What I had been searching for was *text*, 1,500 to 3,000 words of it, three to four consecutive pages of black-and-white print that, in my mind, constituted an article. After all, that's what I'd grown up reading in my father's magazines, in his *Sports Illustrated*, in his *Newsweek*, in his *US News and World Report*.

I put *Outside* back on the rack and grabbed a copy of *Philadelphia Magazine* and encountered the same problem: short, one-page articles decorated with lots of bells and whistles. I made a third attempt, this time grabbing a copy of *Runner's World* but was still disappointed by the lack of text. *I'm so yesterday*, I thought to myself, feeling tragically behind the times. Outside of academic journals, 3,000-word articles were clearly a thing of the past. So were magazines with consecutive pages of nothing but black-and-white text.

This discovery was quite shocking to me, and so I began systematically picking up magazine after magazine at random—*People, Entertainment Weekly, Maxim, Cosmopolitan, Sporting News*—searching the length of the articles, estimating word counts, noting the size and color of the headlines, subheadings, pictures, graphs, and all manner of gimmicks geared toward grabbing the attention of a society of people who watched an average of five hours of TV per day. What I found was disheartening, especially as an English teacher who's spent his life trying to turn kids on to reading. Almost all of these magazines valued flash over substance. Even *Time* and *Newsweek*, the magazines of the intellectual mainstream, weren't what they used to be.

That's when it hit me like a ton of books being thrown into a recycling bin: *America doesn't like to read anymore*. We like to *talk* about reading, especially politicians promising to cure illiteracy, but deep down inside, we don't want to be bothered. For many Americans, reading is uncomfortable. For many Americans, reading is *boring*. For many Americans, if the book doesn't come on audiotape, if it hasn't been made into a movie, if you can't get it on YouTube, if the text isn't broken up into digestible pieces and surrounded with pretty drawings or half-naked pictures of your favorite celebrity, they simply aren't interested.

In their study, *The Family: America's Smallest School*, researchers Barton and Coley report that:

> A comparison of eighth-graders in 45 countries found that U.S. students spend less time reading books for enjoyment and doing jobs at home than students in the average country participating in the study. On the other hand, U.S. eighth-graders spent more time, on average, watching television and videos, talking with friends, and participating in sports activities. They also spend almost one more hour daily using the Internet.[4]

As an English teacher, I've attended dozens of workshops and professional developments on literacy. A major key to improving reading is teaching students that reading is an *active*—not a passive—process. Proficient readers engage with the text as they read it, analyze and reanalyze points and ideas as they come along. They are aware of the organization of the words on the page, the headings, the subheadings, thesis sentences, supporting details, conclusions. They also *make predictions* when they read, which keeps them interested in the passage, keeps them moving forward to the end.

Strong readers—children with natural linguistic abilities and whose parents read to them often during infancy—do these things naturally, without thinking about it. When they read, they unconsciously analyze, predict, organize, and, therefore, comprehend. Struggling readers, on the other hand—children with limited linguistic abilities or who grew up in homes where reading was a rarity—do not engage thoroughly enough with the text they are reading. They run their eyes over the lines and possibly say the words to themselves in their brains (the words that they can understand), but a larger connection is not being made.

To help these children, the teacher must show them how to engage with the text, how to become an *active* reader. This is not an easy task, especially at the high school level, where some children are *years* below grade level. There are a number of strategies aimed at engaging readers—guides to help them analyze and predict—but the interesting part about teaching reading is this: without an attention span, none of it matters. Likewise, without practice, these literacy skills will never adequately take root.

Educators are well aware of these issues. One solution to combat the problem of short attention spans is a strategy called "chunking." Chunking shows students how to break text down into small, digestible pieces; interestingly, the nifty packaging of the magazine articles mentioned above are nothing more than a glorified version of chunking, which speaks volumes about literacy, American pop culture, and the attention span of our nation as a whole. Another solution to help struggling readers focus is to give them shorter passages to work with or provide them with "high interest reading," material that is often big on flash and short on substance, stories beefed up with a lot of gratuitous sex or violence or materialism; the Gossip Girl books by Cecily von Ziegesar are one example of this.

Of course, the literature found in high school curriculums across America is a bit more challenging. It's not so easily chunked or neatly packaged on a single page or pumped-up with charters who get breast implants and drink vodka bongs. This might help explain why some of our children's reading scores are where they are. This might shed some light on why many 11th graders can no longer sit still and read the 672 pages of John Steinbeck's *Grapes of Wrath* or the 704 pages of Herman Melville's *Moby-Dick* or sit for hours at a clip and successfully complete the verbal portion of the PSSA or ACT or SAT.

Tragically, a tug-of-war is going on in education today. On one side is American pop culture, loaded with television and video games and the Internet, a culture of instant gratification and 30-second sound bites. On the other side are our schools, staffed by teachers trying to preserve substance, literacy, and academic merit. In the middle is the child receiving the mixed message. *Why do I need to learn how to read a map, isn't that what a GPS is for? Why do I need to know how to use a dictionary, doesn't my computer have spell check? Huh? I thought you said this was a short story? This is like two-and-a-half pages long!*

If we truly want to increase literacy in school, our society must make an effort to become more literate itself.

EDUCATING CHILDREN CONDITIONED TO VIOLENCE

In 1960, when Alfred Hitchcock's film *Psycho* was released in theaters, America was a different place. One of the reasons Hitchcock decided to shoot *Psycho* in black-and-white was because he thought it would be too gory in color. Interestingly, the "goriest" part of the film was the famous shower scene, which involved no more than a man slashing through a shower curtain with a knife, a woman screaming and raising her hands to block the blows, and blood, which was actually Bosco's chocolate syrup, gurgling down the drain. Nevertheless, the scene shocked and horrified millions of Americans, leaving some, such as my grandmother, outraged and speechless.

That was gore in 1960. Today gore is a bit different. Horror films in the 21st century are beyond graphic, prompting directors to employ special effects crews who can convincingly hack-off heads, explode torsos, drive power drills through chest cavities, and cut legs with chainsaws. In such cases, blood and guts are everywhere, orange-yellow leaking from oozing intestines and dark purple flowing from gushing arteries. If my grandmother were alive today, I wonder what she would think of all this. I wonder how she would react to seeing the movie *Hostel*, or any of the various *Saw* films.

The fact that Americans can stomach such films is partly the result of something called *desensitization*. Desensitization is the process by which people become accustomed to things. When you become *desensitized* to something, it no longer shocks or disturbs you. Many observers of the Rodney King Case, the black motorist beaten by four LA police officers in 1991, suggest the officers were originally acquitted of the crime because the jury had become desensitized to the video of the beating, which was played continuously in slow motion throughout the trial by the defense.

Through television, film, Internet, video games, and music videos, students today have an ample opportunity to develop a high tolerance for violence, not just a tolerance for it, in fact, but a *taste* for it. It's true. I hear my students talking about it all the time. Over the years, I've heard kids in my homeroom passionately discuss the scene in the film *American History X* where the skinhead makes the black guy bite down on the curb and then stomps on the back of his head, killing him (this, by the way, has become known in the urban lexicon as a *curb stomp*). I've heard them brag about their prowess in the video game *Grand Theft Auto*, explaining how they pumped so many people full of holes with a semiautomatic weapon, leaving them to die in a puddle of blood. I've heard them proudly recite the lyrics to their favorite songs, either rap or metal or some hybrid of the two, songs with a message about shooting or killing someone or about back-slapping a bitch across the face because she didn't act right. I've seen them huddle together in their desks and talk about the crazy Internet sites they visit, the ones that show actual footage of real war, real murder, real suicides.

In light of the violent culture of 21st-century America and young people's fascination with it, how should educators proceed with education? How do teachers and schools *compete* with the adrenaline rush of blood and guts and death when it comes to classroom instruction? With so much distraction and desensitization, how do teachers get on a student's radar?

Reading teachers have been fighting this battle for years. The further society pushes the envelope when it comes to violence, the more desensitized youth become. Lessons that were once spicy and provocative slowly become tame and fail to stimulate. Baz Luhrmann's 1996 film *Romeo + Juliet* is a perfect example. Ten years ago, my students sat captivated by the opening scene, which depicted a full-scale gun battle at a gas station between the Motagues and the Capulets. Today, when I show the film to my freshmen, too often they are less than enthused.

This lack of enthusiasm carries over to the literature in many public school textbooks. There's only so much a teacher can do to make Henry David Thoreau's 1848 essay "Civil Disobedience," which was part of the Philadelphia School District's 2009–2010 11th-grade curriculum, fun and interesting. There's only so much a teacher can do to spice up Ralph Waldo Emerson's tedious 1841 essay "Self-Reliance." There's only so much a teacher can do to get 16-year-old inner-city teenagers excited about *The Narrative of the Life of Frederick Douglas*, even when they focus on the bloody fist fight between Douglas and Mr. Covey, the slave master. Teachers might spice up the reading by facilitating discussions about racism, dignity, and self-respect, but ultimately, because teachers need to give their lessons rigor and work on language and critical-thinking skills, students must *read* the story and analyze it through real, structured writing. And this is where many kids begin to tune out.

Group work may help and so might a more hands-on, project-based lesson. These instructional strategies can only get a teacher so far when it comes to literacy, however. Young people must be taught to come out of their comfort zones and accept the fact that academics isn't going to pack the same adrenaline rush as video games, television, or the Internet. Teachers are there to *inform*, not necessarily to entertain. While teachers should work to make lessons interesting, schools must hold fast to academic rigor and fight to undo the negative effects violence is having on learning.

EDUCATING CHILDREN CONDITIONED TO SEX

The same thing that applies to violence applies to sex: American students are developing a real taste for smut. There's no better example of this than the phenomenon known as "sexting," the practice of teens sharing promiscuous photos of themselves and their classmates over their cell phones or sending one another sexually explicit text messages. According to a 2009 article in *Reader's Digest* by Judith Newman, sexting is on the rise. Newman bases her conclusion on a survey conducted by the National Campaign to Prevent Teen and Unplanned Pregnancy and Cosmo Girl.com, who surveyed 1,280 teenagers and young adults about their cell phone and Internet activities. Newman writes:

> According to the survey, one in five girls (11 percent between 13 and 16) and 18 percent of teen boys have sent or posted nude or semi-nude pictures or videos of themselves. About 15 percent of senders forwarded photos to people they hadn't actually met but knew only online. E-mails containing sexual come-ones are even more prevalent: About 39 percent have tapped out lurid e-mails and text messages.[5]

Teen sexting has sparked outrage in many adults, including lawmakers. In 2010, the state of Pennsylvania joined 20 other states to consider laws that would ban teens from sending sexually explicit photos or text. Seth Grove, a state representative from York County, Pennsylvania, led the charge. The goal, according to Grove, wasn't to punish kids for pranks but to protect young people from unintentionally getting themselves into precarious or harmful situations.[6]

Nevertheless, sexting is a clear offshoot of American pop culture. Using nudity to acquire attention and gain social status is a time-honored tradition. It was that famous photo of Marilyn Monroe in the December 1953 inaugural issue of *Playboy*—the one of her sprawled naked across a red velvet backdrop, her right arm stretched above her head, her legs in the fetal position—that first brought smut into the American mainstream.[7]

Jackie Kennedy also did her part. In 1971, while on vacation, she decided to go sunbathing in the nude. A paparazzo got wind of this (rumors circulated he was tipped off by Jackie's second husband, Aristotle Onassis), and a series of photos were taken. Four years later, in August of 1975, these photos ended up in Larry Flint's fledgling *Hustler*, and sales of the magazine exploded.[8]

Other big names have disrobed as well. In February of 1977, nude photos of Arnold Schwarzenegger were published in a magazine called *After Dark*. The theme of the issue was "Musclebound for Glory," and Schwarzenegger posed for the cover shot as well as two inside pictures.[9] In June 1982, Scott Brown, U.S. senator from Massachusetts, did a nude centerfold for *Cosmopolitan*.[10]

Philadelphia School District product Sylvester Stallone is no stranger to nudity. He posed naked in the October 1985 issue of *Playgirl* (an issue that also featured a nude pictorial of boxer Hector "Macho" Camacho).[11] Stallone fans may also remember his more vintage work, when he starred in a 1970, soft-core porn flick called "The Party at Kitty and Stud's," a film that would later, after the success of "Rocky," be renamed "The Italian Stallion."

Kelli McCarty is perhaps the most extreme. Voted Miss USA in 1991, McCarty gradually progressed from beauty pageants to soap operas to a full-blown XXX adult film. Yes, former Miss USA is a now porn star.[12]

But this doesn't seem to faze today's teens. "Among girls and boys, porn has become increasingly accepted, even kind of cool," says Pamela Paul, the author of *Pornified: How Pornography Is Transforming Our Lives, Our Relationships, and Our Families*.[13] And why shouldn't it be cool? The porn culture has trickled down steadily into mainstream America. ABC's primetime show *Wife-Swap*, although an innocent family-oriented program, has a disturbingly suggestive title. So does ABC's *Desperate Housewives*. Desperate for what, exactly? The same goes for ABC's *Cougar Town*, a series about a divorced, middle-aged mom still on the prowl. Then there is Bravo's *The Real Housewives of New Jersey*. (What is America's fetish for housewives?) Interestingly, cougars and housewives and the fantasies about swapping these desperate women all stem from the world of swingers and pornography, as I'm sure the creators of these programs were well aware.

So where does that leave the youth of America? How do schools and America's educational system fare in the face of our country's obsession with sex? Like the problem with the glorification of violence, it leaves teachers in the 21st century struggling to compete for the minds and attention spans of too many students. It's becoming increasingly difficult to turn on the young lady in the back row of my classroom to Shakespeare's *Taming of the Shrew* when she's conditioned to reading Cecily von Ziegesar's *Gossip Girl*, a book about a crew of teens who have a passion for sex, lies, and expensive booze. The excerpt on the back cover of the book sums up the characters general lack of decency: "Welcome to New York City's Upper East Side, where my friends and I live, go to school, play and sleep—sometimes with each other."[14] *Gossip Girl* became a television series on the CW network in 2007, enabling children to watch their favorite materialistic characters in the comfort of their living rooms and skip the reading altogether.

Like the adrenaline rush of violence, youth conditioned to gratuitous sex are no longer responding as well to challenging academic material of substance.

TECHNOLOGY AND TRADITIONAL VALUES

In 2009, Common Sense Media commissioned the Benenson Strategy Group to conduct extensive interviews with teenage students and their parents about the use of digital media for cheating in school. The results of the study were very telling. The report concludes that 83 percent of students had cell phones and that in an average week, teens sent 440 text messages—110 of which were sent during class. Sixty-five percent of teens used their cell phones in the building despite school policy. Thirty-five percent admitted to cheating on a test at least once with their cell phone, while 65 percent said they knew of somebody who had cheated with a cell phone. Shockingly, only 41 percent said that using a cell phone to store and access notes during a test was a serious offense, while 23 percent didn't think it was cheating at all. As for the Internet, 52 percent of teens admitted to using the web for some form of cheating, such as plagiarism. And what did parents think of this? Ninety-two percent said they believed cheating was taking place at their child's school; although, only 3 percent believed it involved their own children.[15]

There have emerged two basic philosophies on handling the problem of cell phones in schools. One is to adopt a policy of zero tolerance—to ban phones from schools altogether. Technically, as of the 2009–2010 school year, the Philadelphia School District had a "no cell phone" policy in their schools. Page 10 of their 2009–2010 Code of Student Conduct describes "possession of beepers, pagers or cell phones, and other electronic devices" as a level-one behavior infraction.[16] However, discretion was ultimately left up to the principals. In special circumstances, cell phones were permitted in schools on an individual basis, as long as they were turned off and stored in a student's locker.

There are those folks, of course, who take a different attitude when it comes to cell phones and schools. There are those who embrace the fact that technology is the wave of the future and clearly here to stay. Education is nearing a point when all schools will be paperless, when the electronic word will replace the printed word, when laptops will serve the function of books. Most teachers do not object to this. There are numerous benefits of the information age, and when used properly, technology can work educational wonders.

Not all educators buy into the idea that cell phones can be tools for classroom learning, however. When you cut through all the rhetoric about technology, cell phones are an *addiction*. A cell phone might be good for accessing the Internet to do research, or it might have other multimedia uses and applications, but there's going to be a time—a *substantial* amount of time—when the cell phone will need to be turned off and put away. That means no answering a quick text message or taking an "emergency" call from a relative. Yet if the phone is right there in the student's pocket or book bag, the student will be tempted to use it. And many students do not have the ability to discipline themselves and use restraint.

Cell phone companies undoubtedly understand this addiction, but they're not going to stop advertising to teens or let disruptions in learning get in the way of making billions of dollars in profit. To ward off complaints by teachers and meet objections from educators before they can be adequately raised, cell phone companies have been very admirably donating a piece of their extremely large profits to education.

Verizon, for example, has started thinkfinity.org, a website that offers free lesson plans and professional development for teachers, after-school activities for children, education news, and the like.[17] To lay it on even thicker, they also launched verizonfoundation.org, a website that boasts of "forging partnerships and focusing on social issues that impact our employees, customers and communities in the areas of education, literacy, safety and health."[18] Verizon even offers educational awards and grants to certain schools.

Not everyone associated with technology is so intent on keeping up a glowing image, however. Some techno-geeks and designers of cell phone applications are simply out to cause a ruckus and make a buck. Baby Shaker, the 2009 Apple multimedia application that allowed users to shake their iPhones and, in the process, silence a crying baby on the screen is one example.[19] Although Apple apologized and removed the program from their website because of complaints from child welfare groups, it's inconceivable why Apple would have placed a game like this on the market in the first place.

For those who thought Baby Shaker was just a harmless gag, they should understand what researchers in early childhood education have been saying for decades: the development of a child's vocabulary and later academic achievement has a direct correlation to their interaction with their parents in infancy. A child who grows up in a home where his parents shake him or shout discouragements (as opposed to a home where his mother and father give verbal encouragements) is more likely to have a lower IQ in school.[20] What does Apple's Baby Shaker say about our society? What does it say about parents and their ability to make their children school ready?

In addition to Baby Shaker, you have SpreadTweet—the 2009 creation for the trendy Twitter, the web-based communication service that allows people to stay connected to friends and celebrities through the exchange of quick, frequent, one-line messages. When you subscribe to someone on Twitter, every time that person sends out a "tweet" (a quick one-line message), you receive the message. If Britney Spears tweets that she's not wearing any underwear, or if Snoop Dog lets it be known he just smoked a big fat blunt, you'll get the message. Now multiply that by 50 celebrities and 75 of your friends, and you'll be getting tweets nonstop, all day long.

But what happens to your Twitter addiction at work, when it's time to head to the office? Well, tech-geeks have got that all figured out. In 2009, a maverick web designer created SpreadTweet, a computer page that looks like a Microsoft Excel spreadsheet. AppScout, a technology website that reviews computer applications and other software, described SpreadTweet this way:

> If you're a Twitter addict but work in an office that doesn't condone your tweeting habits, you have a few options: You could actually do work; you could make yourself paranoid by looking over your shoulder as you post, or you could download SpreadTweet, an Adobe AIR-based Twitter client that looks exactly like a Microsoft Excel Spreadsheet. It'll let you post to Twitter freely, and when the boss walks by behind you, he'll think you're working—as long as he doesn't lean in to see which spreadsheet you're working on.[21]

Baby Shaker and SpreadTweet are just two examples of how technology is having a negative effect on education and work ethic. Of course it's *humans*—not technology—who are to blame for this. People are the ones who *abuse* technology. People are the ones addicted to cell phones and the Internet. People are the ones addicted to computer-generated graphics in movies and video games and chemical pharmaceuticals that help you lose 15 pounds in 30 days without diet or exercise. Technology is just a vice. The real issue that needs examination is America's gradual loss of traditional values.

Traditional values, which transcend race, gender, and politics, is a system of living based on centralized, unchanging principles. Traditional values are *human* values—a roadmap to ensure a person's behavior benefits the common good—and they can be used in any situation, at any time, and in any place. Some traditional values include respect for authority, especially for teachers and elders; respect for the institution of marriage, not in terms of gender but in terms of its being entered into with wisdom and reverence; respect for family and the idea that both mothers and fathers are responsible for making a lifelong commitment to raising their children; honesty and the policy of telling the truth; discipline and work ethic and the ability to honor commitments and meet deadlines; and restraint, the effort to control urges and impulses and to avoid overindulging in sex, materialism, and other such decadent behaviors.

Americans, with their addiction to technology, have been failing to live by many of these principles. Society must take a thorough inventory of its values and priorities in order to give students the moral compass they need to achieve in school.

THE MEDIA AND EDUCATION

In 2001, Bill Kovach and Tom Rosenstiel, two noteworthy and award-winning journalists, published a book called *The Elements of Journalism: What Newspeople Should Know and the Public Should Expect*. The book, which has become required reading in many schools of journalism around the country, was written because Kovach and Rosenstiel felt the art and craft of journalism was steadily going awry. The book began in June of 1997 when 25 of the country's top journalists—the nation's most distinguished writers, editors, and educators—met at the Harvard Faculty Club because they were concerned about the state of journalism in America.

"They were there because they thought something was seriously wrong with their profession," write Kovach and Rosenstiel. "They barely recognized what they considered journalism in much of the work of their colleagues. Instead of serving a larger public interest, they feared, their profession was damaging it."[22]

One of the complaints voiced at the meeting was that editors were being pressured by profit margins, which, in effect, hampered good journalism. Another gripe was that "news was becoming entertainment and entertainment was becoming news."[23] Over the next two years, the group formed the Committee of Concerned Journalists and worked to define journalism and its principal elements in an attempt to improve its quality and bring back a minimum standard of respectability.

The media and its need to entertain in order to survive and turn a profit (more and more newspapers are going bankrupt because Americans don't read anymore) is impacting on education and the way the public perceives it. Stories on "bad teachers" and "failing schools" have become boilerplate, many of them regurgitating the same information, some of which is mishandled and misrepresented. Not that teachers and schools don't have room to improve, but the media's consistent glass-is-half-empty approach to covering education is hurting morale and America's public schools as a whole.

A 2009 editorial in the *Philadelphia Inquirer* headlined "Obama's Plan" shows the generic way newspapers, struggling to survive with ever-shrinking resources and manpower, churn out articles about education void of any real substance, insight, or expertise.

"In his boldest moves, Obama wants to link teacher's pay to student performance and expand the number of charter schools," the *Inquirer* writes. "Those issues go to the heart of what is wrong with the public education system: Too many schools are straddled with bad teachers and too many students with no other choice are stuck in failing schools."[24]

Although there may have been some truth to their argument, the *Inquirer*'s oversimplification of the problems facing education is representative of the way editorial writers operate in the 21st century. The problems facing public education run *much deeper* than teachers and performance pay. Calling out "bad teachers" was a lazy way of filling space and drumming up cheap reaction. If the editorial writers would have dug deeper, if they would have given some new insight on performance pay or provided some interesting facts on ineffectual teachers, then the piece may have been of some value. But they didn't. They just parroted the same shopworn criticisms of public schools—*lousy teachers*—which took no effort on the part of the editorial staff and, for the most part, wasted the precious time of their busy (and dwindling) readers.

Obviously, with so much public scrutiny on bad teachers and schools, there must be some truth to the matter. And of course there is; there are teachers in the system who are burnt out, apathetic, or just plain lack the level of talent and expertise needed to properly manage and educate our nation's children. However, one thing must be said in terms of the media and education: *America's public school system is not nearly as bad as it's made out to be.*

Education is a multibillion-dollar industry. Keeping it broken serves the interest of a wide variety of people and organizations, some of which include testing services, textbook companies, education management organizations, colleges, universities, researchers, social scientists, journalists, legislators, education secretaries, education policy groups, think tanks, lobbyists, community groups, and all manner of nonprofits aimed at helping children learn. Plus, education is great for politicians because it can serve as an all-purpose excuse. There isn't a problem under the sun that can't, in some way, be blamed on education. Crime, poverty, racism, the failing economy—all of these things can be tied back to "bad teachers" and "failing schools."

Using schools as scapegoats is nothing new. It's been going on since at least 1957, when the Russians beat the Americans into space with Sputnik. Although there were many reasons the Russians won round one of the space race—such as the fact that the U.S. neglected ballistic missile development for six years after World War II—both government officials and the media blamed schools.

"None of these reasons had anything to do with what was happening in schools," writes Gerald W. Bracey, noted social scientist, in his book, *Education Hell: Rhetoric vs. Reality*. "It didn't matter. The scapegoating began almost immediately."[25]

And it continued steadily, fueled by a five-part series in *Life* magazine in 1958, the first of which did a comparison between an intelligent, stern-faced Russian boy named Alexei from Moscow, and a soft, grinning American boy named Stephen from Chicago.[26] The article basically laid the groundwork for the premise that Americans were falling behind the Russians because American schools were substandard and produced slackers for students.

"Since *Sputnik*, the driving force of this country, especially in education, has been fear," writes Bracey.[27] Fear that our students are intellectually soft; fear that America is falling behind the rest of the world; fear that our country is failing to produce an adequate amount of engineers and scientists. Curiously, researchers such as Bracey who've crunched the numbers on America's supposed lack of scientists and engineers (an argument numerous presidents have made many times while chastising America's public schools), have found it to be "one of the longest running hoaxes in the country."[28] The reality of the situation is that there *is* no shortage of scientists and engineers in America.

Another misconception purported by politicians and the media is test scores. In particular, the idea that our students are getting "dumber" because of falling SAT scores. In 1990, Richard Cohen, a *Washington Post* columnist, wrote an article titled "Johnny's Miserable SATs," in which he flat out calls American students "dumb" because their average SAT scores were 476 in math and 424 in verbal.[29] However, these kids were only being labeled "dumb" because their test scores were dropping in comparison to those of an elite group of students tested in 1941. According to Bracey, in *Education Hell: Rhetoric vs. Reality*:

> The SAT never represented the scores of the typical student applying to college.... The norms originally were set on a group of 10,654 seniors mostly living in New England and New York. Ninety-eight percent were White; 61% were male; and 41% had attended private, college preparatory high schools.... By 1990, 52% of the seniors were girls, 29% were minorities, and 87% attended public institutions. Many more in 1990 came from low-income families than in the 1941 elite.[30]

Over the years, the media has done much to manipulate the public's perspective on education. If newspapers and magazines truly want to aid learning, they must not only become better informed, but also they must strive for a higher quality of journalism.

NOTES

1. "John Taylor Gatto," The Odysseus Group, www.johntaylorgatto.com/aboutus/john.htm (accessed August 26, 2010).
2. Edward L. Swing, Douglas A. Gentile, Craig A. Anderson, and David A. Walsh, "Television and Video Game Exposure and the Development of Attention Problems," *Pediatrics* 126, no. 2 (August 2, 2010): 214.
3. Alana Semuels, "Television Viewing at All-Time High," *Los Angeles Times*, February 24, 2009.
4. Paul E. Barton and Richard J. Coley, *The Family: America's Smallest School*, (Princeton, NJ: Educational Testing Service, September 2007), 4, www.ets.org/Media/Research/pdf/PICFAMILY.pdf.
5. Judith Newman, "Porn Has Gone Interactive—and Your Kids Are at Risk: From 'Sexting' to Video Chats, How to Fight Back," *Reader's Digest*, May 2009, 120–21.
6. Trish Wilson, "Pa. Working to Outlaw Teen 'Sexting,'" *Philadelphia Inquirer*, August 2, 2010.
7. "What Makes Marilyn?" *Playboy*, December 1953, 17–19.
8. "The Agony, Ecstasy, and Nudity of Jacqueline Kennedy Onassis," *Hustler*, August 1975, 31–37.
9. "Musclebound for Glory," *After Dark*, February 1977, 41.
10. "Cosmo's Centerfold Winners," *Cosmopolitan*, June 1982.
11. "Sylvester Stallone," *Playgirl Magazine*, October 1985, 39.
12. Olga Boyko, "Former Miss USA Kelli McCarty Trades Soap Opera Acting Gig for Porn Role," *New York Daily News*, January 20, 2009, www.nydailynews.com/gossip/2009/01/20/2009-01-20_former_miss_usa_kelli_mccarty_trades_soa.html.
13. Newman, "Porn Has Gone Interactive," 121.
14. Cecily von Ziegesar, *Gossip Girl* (New York: Little, Brown, 2002).
15. "Hi-Tech Cheating: Cell Phones and Cheating in Schools; A National Poll," Benenson Strategy Group and Common Sense Media, 2009, http://msnbcmedia.msn.com/i/MSNBC/Sections/NEWS/PDFs/2010_PDFs/100202_CellPhoneSchoolCheating.pdf.
16. "School District of Philadelphia 2009–2010 Code of Student Conduct," School District of Philadelphia, www.phila.k12.pa.us/offices/administration/policies/CodeofConduct_0910.pdf (accessed August 27, 2010).
17. Thinkfinity, www.thinkfinity.org/.
18. Verizon Foundation, www.verizonfoundation.org/.
19. Suzanne Choney, "'Baby Shaker' App Pulled from iPhone Store," msnbc.com, April 22, 2009, www.msnbc.msn.com/id/30354894/.
20. Betty Hart and Todd R. Risley, *Meaningful Differences in the Everyday Experience of Young American Children* (Baltimore, MD: P. H. Brookes, 1995), 109–11.
21. "SpreadTweet Makes Your Twittering Look Like Work," AppScout, April 22, 2009, www.appscout.com/2009/04/spreadtweet_makes_your_twitter.php (accessed August 27, 2010).
22. Bill Kovach and Tom Rosenstiel, *The Elements of Journalism: What Newspeople Should Know and the Public Should Expect* (New York: Three Rivers, 2001), 10.
23. Kovach and Rosenstiel, *The Elements of Journalism*, 10.
24. Editorial, "Obama's Plan," *Philadelphia Inquirer*, March 13, 2009.
25. Gerald W. Bracey, *Education Hell: Rhetoric vs Reality* (Alexandria, VA: Educational Research Service, 2009), 38.
26. "Schoolboys Point Up a U.S. Weakness," *Life*, March 24, 1958, 26–37.
27. Bracey, *Education Hell*, 121.
28. Bracey, *Education Hell*, 121–22.
29. Richard Cohen, "Johnny's Miserable SATs," *Washington Post*, September 4, 1990.
30. Bracey, *Education Hell*, 68–77.

SEVENTEEN

The Greatest Gift

It takes a village to raise a child. Now, more than ever, it's time to rediscover the truth in this adage. For education to succeed in America, *everyone* must make a conscious effort to contribute. Children must come *first*, and as a nation, we must realize that learning doesn't stop with teachers and schools.

Education is an *active* process. It's admirable to fight for reform, but we can't become too fixated on the idea of waiting for a "superman" that will miraculously transform education in America. Schools do not exist in a vacuum. There is no *in here* and *out there*. The reality is that *we are the system*—all of us—from parents to teachers to professors to politicians. To expect things to change extrinsically is folly. *We* must change, from the inside out, and this can only be done by getting *personally* involved in education, by accepting and understanding our own role in the overall equation.

In the 21st century, it's easy to support education *publicly*. It's easy for corporations to set up educational websites as a vehicle for self-promotion or for film makers to use children and schools as fodder for their documentaries. Likewise, it's easy for politicians to try to win votes by parroting the latest educational rhetoric on the campaign trail.

But what about when the cameras are turned off, when the flashbulbs are done popping, and the election is over? What about when the film, or the human-interest story, or the sales push has ended? What then? How many people care about education on a deeper, more personal level? How many researchers are willing to put aside political correctness in order to ask the questions that truly need exploring? How many entrepreneurs are conscious of the effects their products are having on the attention spans of children? How many professors are teachers first and scholars second? How many parents are reading to their children in infancy, teaching values, and instilling in them the importance of getting an education? How many politicians are well informed about the daily workings of public schools and have thoroughly researched the effects of the policies they are proposing? How many principals and teachers are truly committed to their students and schools?

As an educator, I realize my greatest gift is to teach. The pen may be mightier than the sword, but I know where my ultimate power lies. I know where I can make the greatest difference, where I can have the most impact on the lives of my students, and that is in the classroom. I'm lucky to be in this position. I survived a rocky student-teaching assignment and a challenging first year in the classroom, and finally, through sheer willpower and perhaps a little help from the teaching gods, I eventually came into my own.

Here I stand, a decade and a half later, a *teacher*. Each day, I get up and go to work with the power to change lives. Some days are magical; other days are less than inspiring. This is OK. The world of education is much bigger than little old me. Despite my best efforts, I'm no superman and don't pretend to be. There will be days in the classroom when, despite my best efforts, I may reach one child only—just *one*—but this too is okay; that child's life is changed for the better.

To reach the masses will take the effort of the masses. There is no way around this, for education is a *shared responsibility*. Still, I will do my part and put in my mileage in the classroom. Teaching is where my true power lies. I will forever respect this gift and use it to the best of my ability.

Index

AACTE. *See* American Association of Colleges for Teacher Education
ability levels, 129–130
academic achievement, 148
academic subjects, 29–30
academic tracking: differentiated instruction and, 126; in education, 99–101; poverty and, 99–100
achievement gap: home environment source of, 78; intrinsic and extrinsic solutions to, 86–88; money spent to close, 124; race involved in, 77, 87, 99–100; school inequity issues causing, 78; student work ethic in, 88, 149
Ackerman, Arlene, 36, 38, 63, 136
addiction, to cell phones, 148
admission standards, 10, 21
advisory (homeroom), 52
African Americans, 86
African proverb, xiii
after-class work, of teachers, 54
Alten, Steve, xi
American Association of Colleges for Teacher Education (AACTE), 26
American Educator (Asch), 129
American History X, 144
American Public School Law, 101–102
America's Smallest School: The Family (Barton/Coley), 57
anger management issues, 106
Annual Yearly Progress (AYP), 136
anti-teacher sentiment, 40
articles: short neatly packaged, 141; writing, 115, 116
Asch, Chris Myers, 129
assimilation, cultural, 83–84
attention deficit problems, 106
attention span: of children, 140–143; chunking and, 50, 142; reading and, 136; of students, 142
AYP. *See* Annual Yearly Progress

Baby Shaker, 148–149
Banks, James A., 80, 83
Baraka, Amiri, 84, 85
Barton, Paul E., 57–59, 61, 77, 78, 141–142
BBA. *See* Broader, Bolder Approach to Education
behavior and risks, 57
The Bell Curve: Intelligence and Class Structure in American Life (Herrnstein/Murray), 78
Berla, Nancy, 55
Bill and Melinda Gates Foundation, 39, 45, 104
Black History Month, 84
Boston Latin School, 60
Bracey, Gerald W., 152
Bradbury, Ray, 127
brainstorming, 133
Broader, Bolder Approach to Education (BBA), xiv
Brown, Scott, 146
bulletin board, 18
Bush, George W., 42, 100

California Newsreel, 78–79
Canada, Geoffrey, xiv, 61, 108
Carney, Dana, 125
cell phones, 145; addiction to, 148; Baby Shaker on, 148–149; companies, 148; students cheating with, 147
Center for Parental Leadership, 65
Center on American Progress, 45
Chall, Jeanne, 105
characters, 134
charter schools, 123

Child Poverty in Perspective: An Overview of Child Well-Being in Rich Counties (UNICEF), 56–57
children: academic achievement and, 148; attention spans of, 140–143; communicating with, 7; family and education of, 57–59; Harlem's zone for, xiv; health of, 56–57; must come first, 155; public school nutritional programs for, 63–64; safety of, 56–57; scoring below grade level, 129; self-esteem of, 100; well-being of, 56–57
Christi, Chris, 39, 122
chunking, 50, 142
"Civil Disobedience" (Thoreau), 144
Civil Rights Act, 61
classes, students cutting, 62–63
classroom management: direct instruction in, 104; discipline in, 22; keeping students quiet in, 50; pink slips in, 33–34; seating chart for, 17
classrooms: environment of, 8, 15–16; problems in, 23; students sleeping in, 52–53; teacher-centered, 126
class size: changing, 69; expense of reducing, 42; student achievement influenced by, 40–43
Class-Size Reduction (CSR), 41–42
Class-Size Reduction Program, 41
Clinton, Bill, 40
Cohen, Richard, 152
Coley, Richard J., 57–59, 61, 77, 141–142
Columbia University, xii–xiii
communicating, with children, 7
communities, 60–61
comparisons, 72
comprehensive support assistance programs (CSAPs), 54
Connell, Richard, 24
conservatives, 125, 126, 128
Conwell Middle School placement, 2–4, 4–6
Cooper, Anderson, 108
cooperative learning, 103–107; critics of, 105; defining, 103; direct instruction balance with, 107; in education, 103; student-centered method of, 104–106

core academic subjects, 29–30
Cougar Town, 146
creative writing, 133
CSAPs. *See* comprehensive support assistance programs
CSR. *See* Class-Size Reduction
Cultural Diversity and Education: Foundations, Curriculum and Teaching (Banks), 80, 83
culture: assimilation *v.* pluralism of, 83–84; shock, 31–34; technology changing, 139
Cunningham, George K., 105, 105–106

daily activities, of teachers, 47–54
Danielson, Charlotte, 8
Darling-Hammond, Linda, 43
debates, 4
democrats, republicans *v.*, 123–125
De Niro, Robert, 31
desensitization, 143
Desperate Housewives, 146
The Diary of Anne Frank, 4
Dickens, Charles, 2
Dickey, Eric Jerome, 85
differentiated instruction: academic tracking and, 126; in education, 97–99
A Different Mirror: A History of Multicultural America (Takaki), 79
direct instruction, 103–107; in classroom management, 104; cooperative learning balance with, 107; defining, 103; in education, 103; learning conditions in, 106; teacher-centered method of, 104
discipline, 22
documentaries, 11
Donavan, Rita, 2, 7
Dumbing Us Down: The Hidden Curriculum of Compulsory Schooling (Gatto), 139
Duncan, Arne, 11, 26–27, 136; African American teachers speech of, 86; future teacher motivational speech of, 43; teaching reform speech of, 81
dynamic instructors, 9

Edison Schools, Inc., 121

editorial oversimplification, 151
Ed School Follies: The Miseducation of America's Teachers (Kramer), 21, 82, 121, 128
Educating School Teachers (Levine), 10, 22
education: academic tracking in, 99–101; active process of, 155; Broader, Bolder Approach to, xiv; cell phone companies donating to, 148; conservatives and, 128; cooperative learning in, 103; cultural issues in, 83–84; decline in, 11–12; democrats *v.* republicans in, 123–125; differentiated instruction in, 97–99; direct instruction in, 103; editorial oversimplification about, 151; families' role in, 57–59; high expectations in, 129–130; individualized plans in, 54; least-restrictive environment in, 101; media influencing, 150–152; multicultural, 79–81; multicultural reading in, 79–80; norms of society conformance in, 139; passive approach to, 108; as political scapegoat, 151; politicians making decisions on, 44–45, 121; pop culture competing with, 144; pop culture influencing, 143; in public schools, xiii–xiv; schools of, 21; sex influencing, 145–147; as shared responsibility, 156; socialistic policies in, 128; social justice movement in, 81–83; stakeholders in, 88; stay-put provision in, 102; students involved in, 109–110; technology influencing, 149; urban, 128; violence influencing, 143–145; vocational, 29–30. *See also* schools of education
educational equity, 124, 125, 128–130
educational institution, 57–59
Educational Testing Service, 77
Education Empowerment Act, 122
Education Hell: Rhetoric vs. Reality (Bracey), 152
education management organization (EMO), xiii, 123

Elementary and Secondary Education Act, 61, 124
The Elements of Journalism: What Newspeople Should Know and the Public Should Expect (Kovach/Rosenstiel), 150
Emerson, Ralph Waldo, 144
EMO. *See* education management organization
empowered teachers, 11
English as second language (ESL), 98
ESL. *See* English as second language
ethnic attachments, 83
expense, of reducing class size, 42
extrinsic solutions, 86–88

fact, in news stories, 114
family: children's education and, 57–59; as educational stakeholders, 88. *See also* home environment
The Family: America's Smallest School (Barton/Coley), 141–142
Field, Syd, 133
field experience, 104
figurative language, 71, 73
Finding Mrs. Warnecke: The Difference Teachers Make (Rigsbee), 12
first day teaching, 16–18
five-paragraph essays, 127
Flint, Larry, 146
food insecure, 59
Freire, Paulo, 107

Gatto, John Taylor, 139
gays, 137
Gewertz, Catherine, 121
ghetto, 5
Ginot, Hiam, 7
Giordano, Dom, 40, 42
Gossip Girl (Ziegesar), 142, 146
grade level, 129
Graham, Kristen, 37
Grand Theft Auto, 144
Grapes of Wrath (Steinbeck), 143
Green, Al, 73
Grove, Seth, 145
Guggenheim, Davis, 11
Guns N' Roses, 74

Hardy, Dan, 122
Harlem Children's Zone (HCZ), xiv, 108
Hart, Ann Weaver, xii
Hart, Betty, 55
HCZ. *See* Harlem Children's Zone
health, of U.S. children, 56–57
Henderson, Anne T., 55
"Here's a Radical Idea: Keep Amiri Baraka out of English 101" (Paslay), 85
Herrnstein, Richard J., 78
"The High Cost of Teacher Turnover" (NCTAF), 35
higher socioeconomic school districts, 126
higher standards, 101
Hitchcock, Alfred, 143
Hitler, Adolf, 5
holistic learning process, xiv
Hollywood agencies, 135
Holocaust, 4–5
Holzman, Michael, 86, 99–100
home environment: achievement gap from, 78; as educational institution, 57–59; student achievement impacted by, 55–56
horror films, 143
Howard, Gary R., 80

IDEA. *See* Individuals with Disabilities Education Act
ideology, multicultural, 84
IEPs. *See* individualized education plans
Iglesias, Aquiles, xii
individualized education plans (IEPs), 54, 102
Individuals with Disabilities Education Act (IDEA), 37, 101
"Initiation" (Plath), 32
instant gratification, 143
instructional strategies: five-paragraph essays in, 127; practical, 24–25; in schools of education, 23–24
Intelligence, Genes, and Success: Scientists Respond to "The Bell Curve", 78
internship, in teaching, 2
interviews, 115

intrinsic solutions, 86–88
inverted pyramid, 115

Jacobson, Linda, 43
Jefferson, Thomas, 60
"Johnny's Miserable SATs" (Cohen), 152
Johnson, Lyndon B., 124
journal entries, 49, 51
journalism, 113–117; state of, 150; story angle in, 114
Journal of Political Psychology, 125

Keller, Bess, 104
Kennedy, Dianne, 91, 95
Kennedy, Jackie, 146
King, Martin Luther, Jr., 83
King, Rodney, 143
Kovach, Bill, 150
Kramer, Rita, 21, 82, 121, 128
KWL activity (Know, Want, Learn), 4–5, 23, 49

lack of respect, for teachers, 10–12, 43–45
learning: conditions, 106; different methods of, 103–107; disabled, 102; holistic process of, xiv; teacher and student centered, 125; teacher-centered, 126
least-restrictive environment, 101
lesbians, 137
lesson plans, 19
lessons, interesting, 145
Levine, Arthur, xii, 10, 22–23
liberals, 125, 128
Lincoln High School, 29
literacy, 143
literature, 71, 144
London, Jack, 19
Loveless, Tom, 100–101
low-performing students, 100
Luhrmann, Baz, 144

Madeline Hunter Model, 19
magic trick, 3
Mann, Horace, 60–61
Manzo, Kathleen Kennedy, 107
marriage, same-sex, 137

Maslow, Abraham, 64
McCarty, Kelli, 146
McMillan, Terry, 85
Meaningful Differences in the Everyday Experience of Young American Children (Hart, B./Risley), 55
media: education influenced by, 150–152; public's perspective manipulated by, 152
Melville, Herman, 143
metaphors, 72–75
Miller, Raegen T., 45
Moby-Dick (Melville), 143
money, achievement gap and, 124
Monroe, Marilyn, 145
moral compass, 150
Morrison, Toni, 85
"The Most Dangerous Game" (Connell), 24
movies, 31, 143, 144
multicultural education, 79–81
multicultural ideology, 84
multiculturalism, 74
Murray, Charles, 78, 124, 126, 129
music, diversity of, 74
Myers, Sally, 30

NAEP. *See* National Assessment of Educational Progress
The Narrative of the Life of Frederick Douglas, 144
National Assessment of Educational Progress (NAEP), 77, 101
National Commission on Teaching and America's Future (NCTAF), 35
National Council of Teachers and Mathematics (NCTM), 105
NCTAF. *See* National Commission on Teaching and America's Future
NCTM. *See* National Council of Teachers and Mathematics
A New Generation of Evidence: The Family Is Critical to Student Achievement (Henderson/Berla), 55
Newman, Judith, 145
newspaper, 113–117
news stories, 114
new stories, 115

No Child Left Behind, xiii–xiv, 38, 42, 98, 106, 136
norms of society, 139
nutritional programs, 63–64

Obama, Barack, xiv, 38
"Obama's Plan", 151
Office of Teacher Affairs, 36
O'Flaherty, Liam, 70
opinion, in news stories, 114
Orman, Suze, 11
Outside magazine, 140

Parent Leadership Academy (PLA), 64–65
parents: PLA empowering, 64–65; political involvement and, 64–65; school involvement by, 55, 62–63; teachers dealing with, 47
Parent University, 63
Parsing the Achievement Gap II (Barton/Coley), 59, 78
Paslay, Christopher, 85
passive approach, 108
patience, 51–52
Paul, Pamela, 146
Pedagogy for the Oppressed (Freire), 107
Pennsylvania System of School Assessment (PSSA), 122
performance pay, 38–40, 122
personal responsibility, 107–110
persuasive essays, 137
Philadelphia City Paper, 85, 117
Philadelphia Magazine, 141
Philadelphia Public School Notebook, 64
Philadelphia School District, 63, 124, 129, 147
Phillips, Vicki L., 45
"Philly's Own Al Capone" (Palsay), 117
physical activity, 104
Piccola, Jeffrey E., 122
pink slips, 33–34
Pippet, Margaret M., xii
PLA. *See* Parent Leadership Academy
Plath, Sylvia, 32
Playboy, 145
pluralism, cultural, 83–84
political scapegoat, 151

politics: democrats v. republicans and, 123–125; education decisions and, 44–45, 121; parent's involvement and, 64–65
pop culture, 142; education competing with, 144; education influenced by, 143; instant gratification in, 143; sexting in, 145
Pornified: How Pornography Is Transforming Our Lives, Our Relationships, and Our Families (Paul), 146
pornography, 146
poverty: academic tracking and, 99–100; cycles of, 61
practicality, 23–24
"Precious Lord", 73–74
principals, 22–23, 63
private managers, 122
professional responsibilities, 9
project-based group instruction, 125
protagonist, 133
PSSA. *See* Pennsylvania System of School Assessment
Psycho, 143
public: anti-teacher sentiment of, 40; media manipulating, 152; speaking, 137
public schools: children's nutrition in, 63–64; education in, xiii–xiv; high expectations in, 129–130; Jefferson's vision for, 60; Mann's reform of, 60–61; private managers outperformed by, 122; special education law in, 103; students cutting classes in, 62–63
pyramid, inverted, 115

QNT. *See* quotes, notes, and thoughts
quality teachers, 7–9
The Quest for Quality: Recruiting and Retaining Teachers in Philadelphia (Research for Action), 35
quotes, notes, and thoughts (QNT), 50

race, achievement gap and, 77, 87, 99–100
Race: The Power of an Illusion (California Newsreel), 78

Raging Bull, 31
Reader's Digest, 145
reading: active process of, 142; attention span and, 136; different levels of, 91–96; engagement, 50; multicultural education's required, 79–80; of students, 142; sustained silent, 16
The Real Housewives of New Jersey, 146
Redding, Alice, 15–16
reform, of schools of education, 26–27
relationships, 57, 71
republicans: democrats v., 123–125; teacher-centered classrooms preferred by, 126
Research for Action, 35
resource room, 92
respect, lacking for teachers, 10–12, 43–45
rhetorical skills, 136
Rigsbee, Cindi, 12
Riley, Richard, 40
Ripley, Amanda, 7–8
risks, 57
Risley, Todd R., 55
Robinson, Sharon P., 26–27
role-playing activity, 24
Romeo + Juliet (movie), 144
Romeo and Juliet (Shakespeare), 92–93
Rosenstiel, Tom, 150

safety: of children, 56–57; in schools, 37–38; in U.S., 56–57
same-sex marriage, 137
Sawchuk, Stephen, 39
school districts, 63, 124, 126, 129, 147
schools: achievement gap and inequity issues of, 78; brief history of, 10; charter, 123; communities created by, 60–61; newspaper of, 113–117; parents involved in, 55, 62–63; safety in, 37–38; vouchers used in, 123. *See also specific schools*
schools of education, 21; admission standards of, 21; instructional strategies taught in, 23–24; practical instruction strategies of, 24–25; practicality lacking in, 23–24; principals critical of, 22–23;

reforming, 26–27
Schott Foundation, 77
Schwarzenegger, Arnold, 146
Schweiker, Mark, 121, 124
score proficiency, 138
screenplay, 133–138; brainstorming and, 133; script for, 134; story for, 134; structure of, 133; students writing, 134–135
Screenplay: The Foundations of Screenwriting (Field), 133
script, for screenplay, 134
seating charts, 17, 48
self-esteem, of children, 100
"Self-Reliance" (Emerson), 144
sex, 145–147
sexting, 145
Shakespeare, 92–96, 146
simile, 72–75
sleeping in class, 52–53
social change, 109
socialistic educational policies, 128
social justice: defining, 81; education's movement in, 81–83; implementation of, 82–83; teaching strategies with, 107–108
social responsibility, 107–110
Socratic method of questioning, 4
"Somebody Blew Up America" (Baraka), 84, 85
song lyrics project, 71–75
sonnet, 94–95
Sonnet XVIII (Shakespeare), 93–96
special education law, 103
speeches: of Duncan, 43, 81, 86; motivational, 43
SpreadTweet, 149
Springer, Jerry, 4
SSR. *See* sustained silent reading
stakeholders, in education, 88
Stallone, Sylvester, 146
standardized test scores, 2
staying above the fray, 70
stay-put provision, 102
Steinbeck, John, 143
stereotyping, 83
Stewart Middle School, 15
story, for screenplay, 134
story angle, 114

Stotsky, Sandra, 24, 82, 107
Street, John, 121, 124
structure, students needing, 127
student achievement: class size influencing, 40–43; home environment impact on, 55–56; teacher's performance pay influencing, 38–40, 122
students: ability levels varying of, 129–130; achievement gap and work ethic of, 88, 149; attention spans of, 142; cell phones and cheating by, 147; classroom management quieting, 50; cooperative learning centered on, 104–106; cutting classes, 62–63; different learning methods of, 103–107; educational equity for, 124, 125, 128–130; education involving, 109–110; experiences of, 2; focus on struggling, 92; individual needs of, 97–99; learning centered on, 125; low-performing, 100; moral compass needed by, 150; reading engagement of, 50; reading of, 142; score proficiency of, 138; screenplays written by, 134–135; sleeping in class, 52–53; social change and, 109; structure needed by, 127; teachers forming relationships with, 71; teachers physically assaulted by, 37; teachers relating to, 8; teacher verbally assaulted by, 33–34; teaching experiences with, 2, 18–20; verbal skills of, 126
student-teaching placement, 15
supervisors, 18–20
surgeons, v. teachers, 43–44
sustained silent reading (SSR), 16
Swenson Arts and Technology High School, 113; culture shock teaching at, 31–34; student score proficiency at, 138
Swenson Skills Center, 29
symbolism, 74

Takaki, Ronald, 79
Taming of the Shrew (Shakespeare), 146

Tanner, Dr., 18–20
Tatum, Beverly Daniel, 79, 82
teachers: African American, 86; after-class work of, 54; classroom learning centered around, 126; daily activities of, 47–54; direct instruction centered on, 104; as dynamic instructors, 9; empowering, 11; lack of respect for, 10–12, 43–45; learning centered on, 125; lessons made interesting by, 145; lives changed by, 156; motivational speech to, 43; parents and, 47; patience and temper and, 51–52; performance pay for, 38–40, 122; preserving literacy, 143; professional responsibilities of, 9; quality, 7–9; relating to students, 8; sentiments against, 40; setting higher standards, 101; student attention spans and, 142; students forming relationships with, 71; students physically assaulting, 37; students verbally assaulting, 33–34; surgeons v., 43–44; training of, 21; voice, 4
Teach for America, 8
teaching, 1, 15; Conwell Middle School placement in, 2–4; culture shock, 31–34; differentiated instructions in, 97–99; Duncan's reform speech on, 81; elements of, 97–98; first day, 16–18; internship in, 2; lack of experience in, 24–26; social justice and strategies in, 107–108; song lyrics project and, 71–75; staying above the fray when, 70; student experiences and, 2, 18–20; turnover in, 35–37
technology: cultural changes from, 139; education influenced by, 149
television, 140, 146
temper, 51–52
Temple University, xi–xii
thesis, 118, 127
Thoreau, David, 144
"To Build a Fire" (London), 19
Tomlinson, Carol Ann, 97

Tracking and Detracking: High Achievers in Massachusetts Middle Schools (Loveless), 100
traditional values, 149–150
training, of teachers, 21
turnover, in teaching, 35–37
2007 Guide to Literary Agents, 135

UNICEF, 56–57
United States (U.S.): children's well-being in, 56–57; food insecure and, 59; health and safety in, 56–57; racial achievement gap in, 77, 87, 99–100; relationships ranking of, 57; television watching in, 140
urban education, 128

Vallas, Paul, 36, 117
values, traditional, 149–150
Vento, Joey, 83
verbal skills, 126
Verizon, 148
video games, 140, 144
violence, education and, 143–145
vocabulary words, 70, 98
vocational education, 29–30
von Ziegesar, Cecily, 142, 146
vouchers, school, 123

Waiting for Superman, 11
Walker, Alice, 85
We Can't Teach What We Don't Know: White Teachers, Multicultural Schools (Howard), 80
"Welcome to the Jungle", 74–75
well-being, of children, 56–57
West, Peter, 106
The White-Black Achievement Gap: When Progress Stopped (Educational Testing Service), 77
whole-language movement, 105, 125
Why Are All the Black Kids Sitting Together in the Cafeteria (Tatum), 79, 82
Wife Swap, 146
Williams, Walter E., 21
work ethic, 88, 149

Yarmus, Reuben, xi

Yes We Can (Schott Foundation), 77

Zalot, Morgan, xii

zero tolerance policy, 38

Zogby, Charles B., 121

About the Author

Christopher Paslay teaches high school English in the Philadelphia School District where he's worked since 1997. He's a frequent contributor to the *Philadelphia Inquirer*, where his articles on education and school reform often appear. His commentaries on public schools have also been published in the *Philadelphia Daily News* and the *Philadelphia City Paper*. A believer in the theme of "shared responsibility," Chris continues to advocate for holistic education and serve as a voice for public schoolteachers.

www.ingramcontent.com/pod-product-compliance
Lightning Source LLC
Chambersburg PA
CBHW020830020526
44115CB00029B/101